THE OLD STONE HOUSE AND OTHER STORIES

ANNA KATHARINE GREEN

1st WORLD
LIBRARY
Literary Society

The Old Stone House
and Other Stories

Anna Katharine Green

© 1st World Library, 2007
PO Box 2211
Fairfield, IA 52556
www.1stworldlibrary.com
First Edition

LCCN: 2007934079

Softcover ISBN: 978-1-4218-9614-4
Hardcover ISBN: 978-1-4218-9714-1
eBook ISBN: 978-1-4218-9514-7

Purchase *"The Old Stone House and Other Stories"*
as a traditional bound book at:
www.1stWorldLibrary.com/purchase.asp?ISBN=978-1-4218-9614-4

1st World Library is a literary, educational organization
dedicated to:

- Creating a free internet library of downloadable ebooks

- Hosting writing competitions and offering book publishing
  scholarships.

Interested in more 1st World Library books? contact:
literacy@1stworldlibrary.com
Check us out at: www.1stworldlibrary.com

1ˢᵗ World Library Literary Society

Giving Back to the World

"If you want to work on the core problem, it's early school literacy."

- James Barksdale, former CEO of Netscape

"No skill is more crucial to the future of a child, or to a democratic and prosperous society, than literacy."

- Los Angeles Times

"Literacy... means far more than learning how to read and write... The aim is to transmit... knowledge and promote social participation."

- UNESCO

"Literacy is not a luxury, it is a right and a responsibility. If our world is to meet the challenges of the twenty-first century we must harness the energy and creativity of all our citizens."

- President Bill Clinton

"Parents should be encouraged to read to their children, and teachers should be equipped with all available techniques for teaching literacy, so the varying needs and capacities of individual kids can be taken into account."

- Hugh Mackay

CONTENTS

THE OLD STONE HOUSE........................ 7

A MEMORABLE NIGHT 83

THE BLACK CROSS............................105

A MYSTERIOUS CASE 111

SHALL HE WED HER?.........................120

THE OLD STONE HOUSE

I was riding along one autumn day through a certain wooded portion of New York State, when I came suddenly upon an old stone house in which the marks of age were in such startling contrast to its unfinished condition that I involuntarily stopped my horse and took a long survey of the lonesome structure. Embowered in a forest which had so grown in thickness and height since the erection of this building that the boughs of some of the tallest trees almost met across its decayed roof, it presented even at first view an appearance of picturesque solitude almost approaching to desolation. But when my eye had time to note that the moss was clinging to eaves from under which the scaffolding had never been taken, and that of the ten large windows in the blackened front of the house only two had ever been furnished with frames, the awe of some tragic mystery began to creep over me, and I sat and wondered at the sight till my increasing interest compelled me to alight and take a nearer view of the place.

The great front door which had been finished so many years ago, but which had never been hung, leaned against the side of the house, of which it had almost become a part, so long had they clung together amid the drippings of innumerable rains. Close beside it yawned the entrance, a large black gap through which nearly a century of storms had rushed with their winds and wet till the lintels were green with moisture and slippery with rot. Standing on this untrod threshold, I instinctively glanced up at the scaffolding above me, and started as I noticed that it had partially fallen away, as if time were weakening its supports and making the precipitation of the whole a threatening possibility. Alarmed lest it might fall while I stood there, I did not linger long beneath it, but, with a shudder which I afterwards remembered, stepped into the house and proceeded to inspect its rotting, naked, and unfinished walls. I found them all in the one condition. A fine house had once been planned and nearly completed, but it had been abandoned before the hearths had been tiled, or the wainscoting nailed to its place. The staircase which ran up through the centre of the house was without banisters but otherwise finished and in a state of fair preservation. Seeing this and not being able to resist the temptation which it offered me of inspecting the rest of the house, I ascended to the second story.

Here the doors were hung and the fireplaces bricked, and as I wandered from room to room I wondered more than ever what had caused the desertion of so promising a dwelling. If, as appeared, the first owner had died suddenly, why could not an heir have been found, and what could be the story of a place so abandoned and left to destruction that its walls gave no token of ever having offered shelter to a human being? As I could not answer this question I allowed my imagination full play, and was just forming some weird explanation of the facts before me when I felt my arm suddenly seized from behind, and paused aghast. Was I then not alone in the deserted building? Was there some solitary being who laid claim to its desolation and betrayed jealousy at any intrusion within its mysterious precincts? Or was the dismal place haunted by some uneasy spirit, who with long, uncanny fingers stood ready to clutch the man who presumed to bring living hopes and fears into a spot dedicated entirely to memories? I had scarcely the courage to ask, but when I turned and saw what it was that had alarmed me, I did not know whether to laugh at my fears or feel increased awe of my surroundings. For it was the twigs of a tree which had seized me, and for a long limb such as this to have grown into a place intended for the abode of man, necessitated a lapse of time and a depth of solitude oppressive to think of.

Anxious to be rid of suggestions wellnigh bordering upon the superstitious, I took one peep from the front windows, and then descended to the first floor. The sight of my horse quietly dozing in the summer sunlight had reassured me, and by the time I had recrossed the dismal threshold, and regained the cheerful highway, I was conscious of no emotions deeper than the intense interest of a curious mind to solve the mystery and understand the secret of this remarkable house.

Rousing my horse from his comfortable nap, I rode on through the forest; but scarcely had I gone a dozen rods before the road took a turn, the trees suddenly parted, and I found myself face to face with wide rolling meadows and a busy village. So, then, this ancient and deserted house was not in the heart of the woods, as I had imagined, but in the outskirts of a town, and face to face with life and activity. This discovery was a shock to my romance, but as it gave my curiosity an immediate hope of satisfaction, I soon became reconciled to the situation, and taking the road which led to the village, drew up before the inn and went in, ostensibly for refreshment. This being speedily provided, I sat down in the cosy dining-room, and as soon as opportunity offered, asked the attentive landlady why the old house in the woods had remained so long deserted.

She gave me an odd look, and then glanced aside at an old man who sat doubled up in the opposite corner. "It is a long story," said she, "and I am busy now; but later, if you wish to hear it, I will tell you all we know on the subject. After father is gone out," she whispered. "It always excites him to hear any talk about that old place."

I saw that it did. I had no sooner mentioned the house than his white head lifted itself with something like spirit, and his form, which had seemed a moment before so bent and aged, straightened with an interest that made him look almost hale again.

"I will tell you," he broke in; "I am not busy. I was ninety last birthday, and I forget sometimes my grandchildren's names, but I never forget what took place in that old house one night fifty years ago—never, never."

"I know, I know," hastily interposed his daughter, "you remember beautifully; but this gentleman wishes to eat his dinner now, and must not have his appetite interfered with. You will wait, will you not, sir, till I have a little more leisure?"

What could I answer but Yes, and what could the poor old man do but shrink back into his corner, disappointed and abashed. Yet I was not satisfied, nor was he, as I could see by the appealing glances he gave me now and then from under the fallen masses of his long white hair. But the landlady was complaisant and moved about the table and in and out of the room with a bustling air that left us but little opportunity for conversation. At length she was absent somewhat longer than usual, whereupon the old man, suddenly lifting his head, cried out:

"*She* cannot tell the story. She has no feeling for it; she wasn't *there*."

Anna Katharine Green

"And you were," I ventured.

"Yes, yes, I was there, always there; and I see it all now," he murmured. "Fifty years ago, and I see it all as if it were happening at this moment before my eyes. But she will not let me talk about it," he complained, as the sound of her footsteps was heard again on the kitchen boards. "Though it makes me young again, she always stops me just as if I were a child. But she cannot help my showing you—"

Here her steps became audible in the hall, and his words died away on his lips. By the time she had entered, he was seated with his head half turned aside, and his form bent over as if he were in spirit a thousand miles from the spot.

Amused at his cunning, and interested in spite of myself at the childish eagerness he displayed to tell his tale, I waited with a secret impatience almost as great as his own perhaps, for her to leave the room again, and thus give him the opportunity of finishing his sentence. At last there came an imperative call for her presence without, and she hurried away. She was no sooner gone than the old man exclaimed:

"I have it all written down. I wrote it years and years ago, at the very time it happened. She cannot keep me from showing you that; no, no, she cannot keep me from showing you that." And rising to his feet with a difficulty that for the first time revealed to me the full extent of his infirmity, he hobbled slowly across the floor to the open door, through which he passed with many cunning winks and nods.

"It grows quite exciting," thought I, and half feared his daughter would not allow him to return. But either she was too much engrossed to heed him, or had been too much deceived by his seeming indifference when she last entered the room, to suspect the errand which had taken him out of it. For sooner than I had expected, and quite some few minutes before she came back herself, he shuffled in again, carrying under his coat a roll of yellow paper, which he thrust into my hand with a gratified leer, saying:

"There it is. I was a gay young lad in those days, and could go and come with the best. Read it, sir, read it; and if Maria says anything against it, tell her it was written long before she was born and when I was as pert as she is now, and a good deal more observing."

Chuckling with satisfaction, he turned away, and had barely disappeared in the hall when she came in and saw me with the roll in my hand.

"Well! I declare!" she exclaimed; "and has he been bringing you that? What ever shall I do with him and his everlasting manuscript? You will pardon him, sir; he is ninety and upwards, and thinks everybody is as interested in the story of that old house as he is himself."

"And I, for one, am," was my hasty reply. "If the writing is at all legible, I am anxious to read it. You won't object, will you?"

"Oh, no," was her good-humored rejoinder. "I won't object; I only hate to have father's mind roused on this subject, because he is sure to be sick after it. But now that you have the story, read it; whether you will think as he did, on a certain point, is another question. I don't; but then father always said I would never believe ill of anybody."

Her smile certainly bore out her words, it was so good-tempered and confiding; and pleased with her manner in spite of myself, I accepted her invitation to make use of her own little parlor, and sat down in the glow of a brilliant autumn afternoon to read this old-time history.

*   *   *   *   *

Will Juliet be at home to-day? She must know that I am coming. When I met her this morning, tripping back from the farm, I gave her a look which, if she cares anything about me, must have told her that I would be among the lads who would be sure to pay her their respects at early candle-light. For I cannot resist her saucy pout and dancing dimples any longer. Though I am barely twenty, I am a man, and one who is quite forehanded and able to take unto himself a wife. Ralph Urphistone has both wife and babe, and he was only twenty-one last August. Why, then, should I not go courting, when the prettiest maid that has graced the town for many a year holds out the guerdon of her smiles to all who will vie for them?

To be sure, the fact that she has more than one wooer already may be considered detrimental to my success. But love is fed by rivalry, and if Colonel Schuyler does not pay her his addresses, I think my chances may be considered as good as any one's. For am I not the tallest and most straightly built man in town, and have I not a little cottage all my own, with the neatest of gardens behind it, and an apple-tree in front whose blossoms hang ready to shower themselves like rain upon the head of her who will enter there as a bride? It is not yet dark, but I will forestall the sunset by a half hour and begin my visit now. If I am first at her gate, Lemuel Phillips may look less arrogant when he comes to ask her company to the next singing school.

*   *   *   *   *

I was not first at her gate; two others were there before me. Ah, she is prettier than ever I supposed, and chirper than the sparrow which builds every year a nest in my old apple-tree. When she saw me come up the walk, her cheeks turned pink, but I do not know if it was from pleasure or annoyance, for she gave nothing but vexing replies to every compliment I paid her. But then Lemuel Phillips fared no better; and she was so bitter-sweet to Orrin Day that he left in a huff and vowed he would never step across her threshold again. I thought she was a trifle more serious after he had gone, but when a woman's eyes are as bright as hers, and the frowns and smiles with which she disports herself chase each other so rapidly over a face both mischievous and charming, a man's judgment goes astray, and he scarcely knows reality from seeming. But true or false, she is pretty as a harebell and bright as glinting sunshine; and I mean to marry her, if only Colonel Schuyler will hold himself aloof.

Colonel Schuyler may hold himself aloof, but he is a man like the rest of us for all that. Yesterday as I was sauntering in the churchyard waiting for the appearance of a certain white-robed figure crowned by the demurest of little hats, I caught a glimpse of his face as he leaned on one of the tombstones near Patience Goodyear's grave, and I saw that he was waiting also for the same white figure and the same demure hat. This gave me a shock; for though I had never really dared to hope he would remain unmoved by a loveliness so rare in our village, and indeed, as I take it, in any village, I did not think he would show so much impatience, or await her appearance with such burning and uncontrollable ardor.

Indeed I was so affected by his look that I forgot to watch any longer for her coming, but kept my gaze fixed on his countenance, till I saw by the change which rapidly took place in it that she had stepped out of the great church door and was now standing before us, making the sunshine more brilliant by her smiles, and the spring the sweeter for her presence.

Anna Katharine Green

Then I came to myself and rushed forward with the rest of the lads. Did he follow behind us? I do not think so, for the rosy lips which had smiled upon us with so airy a welcome soon showed a discontented curve not to be belied by the merry words that issued from them, and when we would have escorted her across the fields to her father's house, she made a mocking curtsy, and wandered away with the ugliest old crone who mouths and mumbles in the meeting-house. Did she do this to mock us or him? If to mock him he had best take care, for beauty scorned is apt to grow dangerous. But perhaps it was to mock us? Well, well, there would be nothing new in that; she is ever mocking us.

* * * * *

They say the Colonel passes her gate a dozen times a day, but never goes in and never looks up. Is he indifferent then? I cannot think so. Perhaps he fears her caprices and disapproves of her coquetry. If that is so, she shall be my wife before he wakens to the knowledge that her coquetry hides a passionate and loving heart.

Colonel Schuyler is a dark man. He has eyes which pierce you, and a smile which, if it could be understood, might perhaps be less fascinating than it is. If she has noticed his watching her, the little heart that flutters in her breast must have beaten faster by many a throb. For he is the one great man within twenty miles, and so handsome and above us all that I do not know of a woman but Juliet whose voice does not sink a tone lower whenever she speaks of him. But he is a proud man, and seems to take no notice of any one. Indeed he scarcely appears to live in our world. Will he come down from his high estate at the beck of this village beauty? Many say not, but I say yes; with those eyes of his he cannot help it.

* * * * *

Juliet is more capricious than ever. Lemuel Phillips for one is tired of it, and imitating Orrin Day, bade her a good-even to-night which I am sure he does not intend to follow with a blithe good-morrow.

I might do the same if her pleading eyes would let me. But she seems to cling to me even when she is most provokingly saucy; and though I cannot see any love in her manner, there is something in it very different from hate; and this it is which holds me. Can a woman be too pretty for her own happiness, and are many lovers a weariness to the heart?

* * * * *

Juliet is positively unhappy. To-day when she laughed the gayest it was to hide her tears, and no one, not even a thoroughly spoiled beauty, could be as wayward as she if there were not some bitter arrow rankling in her heart. She was riding down the street on a pillion behind her father, and Colonel Schuyler, who had been leaning on the gate in front of his house, turned his back upon her and went inside when he saw her coming. Was this what made her so white and reckless when she came up to where I was standing with Orrin Day, and was it her chagrin at the great man's apparent indifference which gave that sharp edge to the good-morning with which she rode haughtily away? If it was I can forgive you, my lady-bird, for there is reason for your folly if I am any judge of my fellow-men. Colonel Schuyler is not indifferent but circumspect, and circumspection in a lover is an insult to his lady's charms.

* * * * *

She knows now what I knew a week ago. Colonel Schuyler

Anna Katharine Green

is in love with her and will marry her if she does not play the coquette with him. He has been to her house and her father already holds his head higher as he paces up and down the street. I am left in the lurch, and if I had not foreseen this end to my hopes, might have been a very miserable man to-night. For I was near obtaining the object of my heart, as I know from her own lips, though the words were not intended for my ears. You see I was the one who surprised him talking with her in the garden. I had been walking around the place on the outer side of the wall as I often did from pure love for her, and not knowing she was on the other side was very much startled when I heard her voice speaking my name; so much startled that I stood still in my astonishment and thus heard her say:

"Philo Adams has a little cottage all his own and I can be mistress of it any day,—or so he tells me. I had rather go into that little cottage where every board I trod on would be my own, than live in the grandest room you could give me in a house of which I would not be the mistress."

"But if I make a home for you," he pleaded, "grand as my father's, but built entirely for you—"

"Ah!" was her soft reply, "that might make me listen to you, for I should then think you loved me."

The wall was between us, but I could see her face as she said this as plainly as if I had been the fortunate man at her side. And I could see his face too, though it was only in fancy I had ever beheld it soften as I knew it must be softening now. Silence such as followed her words is eloquent, and I feared my own passions too much to linger till it should be again broken by vows I had not the courage to hear. So I crept away conscious of but one thing, which was that my dream was ended, and that my brave apple-tree would never shower its bridal blossoms upon the head I love, for whatever threshold she crosses as mistress it will not now be that of the little cottage every board of which might have been her own.

* * * * *

If I had doubted the result of the Colonel's offer to Juliet, the news which came to me this morning would have convinced me that all was well with them and that their marriage was simply a matter of time. Ground has been broken in the pleasant opening on the verge of the forest, and carts and men hired to bring stone for the fine new dwelling Colonel Schuyler proposes to rear for himself. The whole town is agog, but I keep the secret I surprised, and only Juliet knows that I am no longer deceived as to her feelings, for I did not go to see her to-night for the first time since I made up mind that I would have her for my wife. I am glad I restrained myself, for Orrin Day, who had kept his word valiantly up to this very day, came riding by my house furiously a half hour ago, and seeing me, called out:

"Why didn't you tell me she had a new adorer? I went there to-night and Colonel Schuyler sat at her side as you and I never sat yet, and—and—" he stammered frantically, "*I did not kill him.*"

"You—Come back!" I shouted, for he was flying by like the wind. But he did not heed me nor stop, but vanished in the thick darkness, while the lessening sound of his horse's hoofs rang dismally back from the growing distance.

So this man has loved her passionately too, and the house which is destined to rise in the woods will throw a shadow over more than one hearthstone in this quiet village. I declare I am sorry that Orrin has taken it so much to heart, for he has a proud and determined spirit, and will not forget his wrongs as soon as it would be wise for him to do. Poor, poor Juliet, are you making enemies against your bridal day? If so, it behooves me at least to remain your friend.

* * * * *

I saw Orrin again to-day, and he looks like one haunted. He was riding as usual, and his cloak flew out behind him as he sped down the street and away into the woods. I wonder if she too saw him, from behind her lattice. I thought I detected the curtain move as he thundered by her gate, but I am so filled with thoughts of her just now that I cannot always trust my judgment. I am, however, sure of one thing, and that is that if Colonel Schuyler and Orrin meet, there will be trouble.

* * * * *

I never thought Orrin handsome till to-day. He is fair, and I like dark men; and he is small, and I admire men of stature. But when I came upon him this morning, talking and laughing among a group of lads like ourselves, I could not but see that his blue eye shone with a fire that made it as brilliant as any dark one could be, and that in his manner, verging as it did upon the reckless, there was a spirit and force which made him look both dangerous and fascinating. He was haranguing them on a question of the day, but when he saw me he stepped out of the crowd, and, beckoning me to follow him, led the way to a retired spot, where, the instant we were free from watching eyes, he turned and said: "You liked her too, Philo Adams. I should have been willing if you—" Here he choked and paused. I had never seen a face so full of fiery emotions. "No, no, no," he went on, after a moment of silent struggle; "I could not have borne it to see any man take away what was so precious to me. I—I—I did not know I cared for her so much," he now explained, observing my look of surprise. "She teased me and put me off, and coquetted with you and Lemuel and whoever else happened to be at her side till I grew beside myself and left her, as I thought, forever. But there are women you can leave and women you cannot, and when I found she teased and fretted me more at a distance than when she was under my very eye, I went back only to find—Philo, do you think he will marry her?"

I choked down my own emotions and solemnly answered: "Yes, he is building her a home. You must have seen the stones that are being piled up yonder on the verge of the forest."

He turned, glared at me, made a peculiar sound with his lips, and then stood silent, opening and closing his hands in a way that made my blood run chill in spite of myself.

"A house!" he murmured, at last; "I wish I had the building of that house!"

The tone, the look he gave, alarmed me still further.

"You would build it well!" I cried. It was his trade, the building of houses.

"I would build it slowly," was his ominous answer.

* * * * *

Juliet certainly likes me, and trusts me, I think, more than any other of the young men who used to go a-courting her. I have seen it for some time in the looks she has now and then given me across the meeting-house during the long sermon on Sunday mornings, but to-day I am sure of it. For she has spoken to me, and asked me—But let me tell you how it was: We were all standing under Ralph Urphistone's big tree, looking at his little one toddling over the grass after a ball one of the lads had thrown after her, when I felt the slightest touch on my arm, and, glancing round, saw Juliet.

She was standing beside her father, and if ever she looked pretty it was just then, for the day was warm and she had taken off her great hat so that the curls flew freely around her face that was dimpled and flushed with some feeling which did not allow her to lift her eyes. Had she touched me? I thought so, and yet I did not dare to take it for granted, for Colonel Schuyler was standing on the edge of the crowd, frowning in some displeasure at the bare head of his provoking little betrothed, and when Colonel Schuyler frowns there is no man of us but Orrin who would dare approach the object of his preference, much less address her, except in the coldest courtesy.

But I was sure she had something to say to me, so I lingered under the tree till the crowd had all dispersed and Colonel Schuyler, drawn away by her father, had left us for a moment face to face. Then I saw I was right.

"Philo," she murmured, and oh, how her face changed! "you are my friend, I know you are my friend, because you alone out of them all have never given me sharp words; will you, will you do something for me which will make me less miserable, something which may prevent wrong and trouble, and keep Orrin—"

Orrin? did she call him Orrin?

"Oh," she cried, "you have no sympathy. You—"

"Hush!" I entreated. "You have not treated me well, but I am always your friend. What do you want me to do?"

She trembled, glanced around her in the pleasant sunshine, and then up into my face.

"I want you," she murmured, "to keep Orrin and Colonel Schuyler apart. You are Orrin's friend; stay with him, keep by him, do not let him run alone upon his enemy, for—for there is danger in their meeting—and—and—"

She could not say more, for just then her father and the Colonel came back, and she had barely time to call up her dimples and toss her head in merry banter before they were at her side.

As for myself, I stood dazed and confused, feeling that my six feet made me too conspicuous, and longing in a vague and futile way to let her know without words that I would do what she asked.

And I think I did accomplish it, though I said nothing to her and but little to her companions. For when we parted I took the street which leads directly to Orrin's house; and when Colonel Schuyler queried in his soft and gentlemanlike way why I left them so soon, I managed to reply:

"My road lies here"; and so left them.

*   *   *   *   *

I have not told Orrin what she said, but I am rarely away from his vicinity now, during those hours when he is free to come and go about the village. I think he wonders at my persistent friendship, sometimes, but he says nothing, and is not even disagreeable to—*me*. So I share his pleasures, if they are pleasures, expecting every day to see him run across

Anna Katharine Green

the Colonel in the tavern or on the green; but he never does, perhaps because the Colonel is always with her now, and we are not nor are ever likely to be again.

Do I understand her, or do I understand Orrin, or do I even understand myself? No, but I understand my duty, and that is enough, though it is sometimes hard to do it, and I would rather be where I could forget, instead of being where I am forced continually to remember.

*   *   *   *   *

Am I always with Orrin when he is not at work or asleep? I begin to doubt it. There are times when there is such a change in him that I feel sure he has been near her, or at least seen her, but where or how, I do not know and cannot even suspect. He never speaks of her, not now, but he watches the house slowly rising in the forest, as if he would lay a spell upon it. Not that he visits it by daylight, or mingles with the men who are busy laying stone upon stone; no, no, he goes to it at night, goes when the moon and stars alone shed light upon its growing proportions; and standing before it, seems to count each stone which has been added through the day, as if he were reckoning up the months yet remaining to him of life and happiness.

I never speak to him during these expeditions. I go with him because he does not forbid me to do so, but we never exchange a word till we have left the forest behind us and stand again within the village streets. If I did speak I might learn something of what is going on in his bitter and burning heart, but I never have the courage to do so, perhaps because I had rather not know what he plans or purposes.

She is not as daintily rounded as she was once. Her cheek is thinner, and there is a tremulous move to her lip I never saw in it in the old coquettish days. Is she not happy in her betrothal, or are her fears of Orrin greater than her confidence in me? It must be the latter, for Colonel Schuyler is a lover in a thousand, and scarcely a day passes without some new evidence of his passionate devotion. She ought to be happy, if she is not, and I am sure there is not another woman in town but would feel herself the most favored of her sex if she had the half of Juliet's prospects before her. But Juliet was ever wayward; and simply because she ought to increase in beauty and joy, she pales and pines and gets delicate, and makes the hearts of her lovers grow mad with fear and longing.

* * * * *

Where have I been? What have I seen, and what do the events of this night portend? As Orrin and myself were returning from our usual visit to the house in the woods—it is well up now, and its huge empty square looms weirdly enough in the moonlighted forest,—we came out upon the churchyard in front of the meeting-house, and Orrin said:

"You may come with me or not, I do not care; but I am going in amongst these graves. I feel like holding companionship with dead people to-night."

"Then so do I," said I, for I was not deceived by his words. It was not to hold companionship with the dead, but with the living, that he chose to linger there. The churchyard is in a direct line with her house, and, sitting on the meeting-house steps one can get a very good view of the windows of her room.

"Very well," he sighed, and disdained to say more.

As for myself, I felt too keenly the weirdness of the whole

situation to do more than lean my back against a tree and wait till his fancy wearied of the moonlight and silence. The stones about us, glooming darkly through the night, were not the most cheerful of companions, and when you add to this the soughing of the willows and the flickering shadows which rose and fell over the face of the meeting-house as the branches moved in the wind, you can understand why I rather regretted the hitherto gloomy enough hour we were accustomed to spend in the forest.

But Orrin seemed to regret nothing. He had seated himself where I knew he would, on the steps of the meeting-house, and was gazing, with chin sunk in his two hands, down the street where Juliet dwelt. I do not think he expected anything to happen; I think he was only reckless and sick with a longing he had not the power to repress, and I watched him as long as I could for my own inner sickness and longing, and when I could watch no longer I turned to the gnomish gravestones that were no more motionless or silent than he.

Suddenly I felt myself shiver and start, and, turning, beheld him standing erect, a black shadow against the moonlighted wall behind him. He was still gazing down the street but no longer in apathetic despair, but with quivering emotion visible in every line of his trembling form. Reaching his side, I looked where he looked, and saw Juliet—it must have been Juliet to arouse him so,—standing with some companion at the gate in the wall that opens upon the street. The next moment she and the person with her stepped into the street, and, almost before we realized it, they began to move towards us, as if drawn by some power in Orrin or myself, straight, straight to this abode of death and cold moonbeams.

It was not late, but the streets were otherwise deserted, and we four seemed to be alone in the whole world. Breathing with Orrin and almost clasping his hand in my oneness with him, I watched and watched the gliding approach of the two lovers, and knew not whether to be startled or satisfied when I saw them cross to the churchyard and enter where we had entered ourselves so short a time before. For us all to meet, and meet here, seemed suddenly strangely natural, and I hardly knew what Orrin meant when he grasped me forcibly by the arm and drew me aside into the darkest of the dark shadows which lay in the churchyard's farthest corner.

Not till I perceived Juliet and the Colonel halt in the moonlight did I realize that we were nothing to them, and that it was not our influence but some purpose or passion of their own which had led them to this gruesome spot.

The place where they had chosen to pause was at the grave of old Patience Goodyear, and from the corner where we stood we could see their faces plainly as they turned and looked at each other with the moonbeams pouring over them. Was it fancy that made her look like a wraith, and he like some handsome demon given to haunting churchyards? Or was it only the sternness of his air, and the shrinking timidity of hers, which made him look so dark and she so pallid.

Orrin, who stood so close to me that I could hear his heart beat as loudly as my own, had evidently asked himself the same question, for his hand closed spasmodically on mine, as the Colonel opened his lips, and neither of us dared so much as to breathe lest we should lose what the lovers had to say.

But the Colonel spoke clearly, if low, and neither of us could fail to hear him as he said:

"I have brought you here, Juliet mine, because I want to hear you swear amongst the graves that you will be no man's wife but mine."

"But have I not already promised?" she protested, with a gentle uplift of her head inexpressibly touching in one who had once queened it over hearts so merrily.

"Yes, you have promised, but I am not satisfied. I want you to swear. I want to feel that you are as much mine as if we had stood at the altar together. Otherwise how can I go away? How can I leave you, knowing there are three men at least in this town who would marry you at a day's notice, if you gave them full leave. I love you, and I would marry you to-night, but you want a home of your own. Swear that you will be my wife when that home is ready, and I will go away happy. Otherwise I shall have to stay with you, Juliet, for you are more to me than renown, or advancement, or anything else in all God's world."

"I do not like the graves; I do not want to stay here, it is so late, so dark," she moaned.

"Then swear! Lay your hand on Mother Patience's tombstone, and say, 'I will be your wife, Richard Schuyler, when the house is finished which you are building in the woods'; and I will carry you back in my arms as I carry you always in my heart."

But though Orrin clinched my arm in apprehension of her answer, and we stood like two listening statues, no words issued from her lips, and the silence grew appalling.

"Swear!" seemed to come from the tombs; but whether it was my emotion that made it seem so, or whether it was Orrin who threw his voice there, I did not know then and I do not know now. But that the word did not come from the Colonel was evident from the startled look he cast about him and from the thrill which all at once passed over her form from her shrouded head to her hidden feet.

"Do the heavens bid me?" she murmured, and laid her hand without hesitation on the stone before her, saying, "I swear by the dead that surround us to be your wife, Richard Schuyler, when the house you are building for me in the woods is completed." And so pleased was he at the readiness with which she spoke that he seemed to forget what had caused it, and caught her in his arms as if she had been a child, and so bore her away from before our eyes, while the man at my side fought and struggled with himself to keep down the wrath and jealousy which such a sight as this might well provoke in one even less passionate and intemperate than himself.

When the one shadow which they now made had dissolved again into two, and only Orrin and myself were left in that ghostly churchyard, I declared with a courage I had never before shown:

"So that is settled, Orrin. She will marry the Colonel, and you and I are wasting time in these gloomy walks."

To which, to my astonishment, he made this simple reply, "Yes, we are wasting time"; and straightway turned and left the churchyard with a quick step that seemed to tell of some new and fixed resolve.

* * * * *

Colonel Schuyler has been gone a week, and to-night I summoned up courage to call on Juliet's father. I had no longer any right to call upon *her*; but who shall say I may not call on him if he chooses to welcome me and lose his time on my account. The reason for my going is not far to seek. Orrin has been there, and Orrin cannot be trusted in her presence alone. Though he seems to have accepted his fate, he is restless, and keeps his eye on the ground in a brooding way I do not comprehend and do not altogether like. Why should he think so much, and why should he go to her house when he knows the sight of her is inflaming to his heart and death to his self-control?

Juliet's father is a simple, proud old man who makes no attempt to hide his satisfaction at his daughter's brilliant prospects. He talked mainly of *the house*, and if he honored Orrin with half as much of his confidence on that subject as he did me, then Orrin must know many particulars about its structure of which the public are generally ignorant. Juliet was not to be seen—that is, during the first part of the evening, but towards its close she came into the room and showed me that same confiding courtesy which I have noticed in her ever since I ceased to be an aspirant for her hand. She was not so pale as on that weird night when I saw her in the churchyard, and I thought her step had a light spring in it which spoke of hope. She wore a gown which was coquettishly simple, and the fresh flower clinging to her bosom breathed a fragrance that might have intoxicated a man less determined to be her friend. Her father saw us meet without any evident anxiety; and if he was as complacent to Orrin when he was here, then Orrin had a chance to touch her hand.

But was he as complacent to Orrin? That I could not find out. I am only sure that I will be made welcome there again *if* I confine my visits to the father and do not seek anything more from Juliet than that simple touch of her hand.

*　*　*　*　*

Orrin has not repeated his visit, but I have repeated mine. Why? Because I am uneasy. Colonel Schuyler's house does not progress, and whether there is any connection between this fact and that of Orrin's sudden interest in the sawmills and quarries about here, I cannot tell, but doubts of his loyalty will rise through all my friendship for him, and I cannot keep away from Juliet any longer.

Does Juliet care for Colonel Schuyler? I have sometimes thought no, and I have oftener thought yes. At all events she trembles when she speaks of him, and shows emotion of no slight order when a letter of his is suddenly put in her hand. I wish I could read her pretty, changeful face more readily. It would be a comfort for me to know that she saw her own way clearly, and was not disturbed by Orrin's comings and goings. For Orrin is not a safe man, I fear, and a faith once pledged to Colonel Schuyler should be kept.

I do not think Juliet understands just how great a man Colonel Schuyler promises to be. When her father told me to-night that his daughter's betrothed had been charged with some very important business for the Government, her pretty lip pouted like a child's. Yet she flushed, and for a minute looked pleased when I said, "That is a road which leads to Washington. We shall hear of you yet as being presented at the White House."

I think her father anticipates the same. For he told me a few minutes later that he had sent for tutors to teach his daughter music and the languages. And I noticed that at this she pouted again, and indeed bore herself in a way which promised less for her future learning than for that influence which breathes from gleaming eyes and witching smiles. Ah, I fear she is a frivolous fairy, but how pretty she is, and how dangerously captivating to a man who has once allowed himself to study her changes of feeling and countenance. When I came away I felt that I had gained nothing, and lost—what? Some of the complacency of spirit which I had acquired after much struggle and stern determination.

*   *   *   *   *

Colonel Schuyler has not yet returned, and now Orrin has gone away. Indeed, no one knows where to find him nowadays, for he is here and there on his great white horse, riding off one day and coming back the next, ever busy, and, strange to say, always cheerful. He is making money, I hear, buying up timber and then selling it to builders, but he does not sell to one builder, whose house seems to suffer in consequence. Where is the Colonel, and why does he not come home and look after his own?

I have learned her secret at last, and in a strange enough way. I was waiting for her father in his own little room, and as he did not come as soon as I anticipated, I let my secret despondency have its way for a moment, and sat leaning forward, with my head buried in my hands. My face was to the fire and my back to the door, and for some reason I did not hear it open, and was only aware of the presence of another person in the room by the sound of a little gasp behind me, which was choked back as soon as it was uttered. Feeling that this could come from no one but Juliet, I for some reason hard to fathom sat still, and the next moment became conscious of a touch soft as a rose-leaf settle on my hair, and springing up, caught the hand which had given it, and holding it firmly in mine, gave her one look which made her chin fall slowly on her breast and her eyes seek the ground in the wildest distress and confusion.

"Juliet—" I began.

But she broke in with a passion too impetuous to be restrained:

"Do not—do not think I knew or realized what I was doing. It was because your head looked so much like his as you sat leaning forward in the firelight that I—I allowed myself one little touch just for the heart's ease it must bring. I—I am so lonesome, Philo, and—and—"

I dropped her hand. I understood the whole secret now. My hair is blonde like Orrin's, and her feelings stood confessed, never more to be mistaken by me.

"You love Orrin!" I gasped; "you who are pledged to Colonel Schuyler!"

"I love Orrin," she whispered, "and I am pledged to Colonel Schuyler. But you will never betray me," she said.

"I betray you?" I cried, and if some of the bitterness of my own disappointed hopes crept into my tones, she did not seem to note it, for she came quite close to my side and looked up into my face in a way that almost made me forget her perfidy and her folly. "Juliet," I went on, for I felt never more strongly than at this moment that I should act a brother's part towards her, "I could never find it in my heart to betray you, but are you sure that you are doing wisely to betray the Colonel for a man no better than Orrin. I—I know you do not want to hear me say this, for if you care for him you must think him good and noble, but Juliet, I know him and I know the Colonel, and he is no more to be compared with the man you are betrothed to than—"

"Hush!" she cried, almost commandingly, and the airy, dainty, dimpled creature whom I knew seemed to grow in stature and become a woman, in her indignation; "you do not know Orrin and you do not know the Colonel. You shall not draw comparisons between them. I will have you think of Orrin only, as I do, day and night, ever and always."

"But," I exclaimed, aghast, "if you love him so and despise

Anna Katharine Green

the Colonel, why do you not break your troth with the latter?"

"Because," she murmured, with white cheeks and a wandering gaze, "I have sworn to marry the Colonel, and I dare not break my oath. Sworn to be his wife when the house he is building is complete; and the oath was on the graves of the dead; *on the graves of the dead!*" she repeated.

"But," I said, without any intimation of having heard that oath, "you are breaking that oath in private with every thought you give to Orrin. Either complete your perjury by disowning the Colonel altogether, or else give up Orrin. You cannot cling to both without dishonor; does not your father tell you so?"

"My father—oh, he does not know; no one knows but you. My father likes the Colonel; I would never think of telling him."

"Juliet," I declared solemnly, "you are on dangerous ground. Think what you are doing before it is too late. The Colonel is not a man to be trifled with."

"I know it," she murmured, "I know it," and would not say another word or let me.

And so the burden of this new apprehension is laid upon me; for happiness cannot come out of this complication.

* * * * *

Where is Orrin, and what is he doing that he stays so much from home? If it were not for the intent and preoccupied look which he wears when I do see him, I should think that he was absenting himself for the purpose of wearing out his unhappy passion. But the short glimpses I have had of him as he has ridden busily through the town have left me with no such hope, and I wait with feverish impatience for some fierce action on his part, or what would be better, the Colonel's return. And the Colonel must come back soon, for nothing goes well in a long absence, and his house is almost at a standstill.

* * * * *

Colonel Schuyler has come and, I hear, is storming angrily over the mishaps that have delayed the progress of his new dwelling. He says he will not go away again till it is completed, and has been riding all the morning in every direction, engaging new men to aid the dilatory workmen already employed. Does Orrin know this? I will go down to his house and see.

* * * * *

And now I know *Orrin's* secret. He was not at home, of course, and being determined to get at the truth of his mysterious absences, I mounted a horse of my own and rode off to find him.

Why I took this upon myself, or whether I had the right to do it, I have not stopped to ask. I went in the direction he had last gone, and after I had ridden through two villages I heard of him as having passed still farther east some two hours before.

Not in the least deterred, I hurried on, and having threaded a thicket and forded a stream, I came upon a beautiful open country wholly new to me, where, on the verge of a pleasant glade and in full view of a most picturesque line of hills, I saw shining the fresh boards of a new cottage. Instantly the thought struck me, "It is Orrin's, and he is building it for Juliet," and filled with a confusion of emotions, I spurred on my horse, and soon drew up before it.

Orrin was standing, pale and defiant, in the doorway, and as I met his eye, I noticed, with a sick feeling of contempt, that he swung the whip he was holding smartly against his leg in what looked like a very threatening manner.

"Good-evening, Orrin," I cried. "You have a very pleasant site here—preferable to the Colonel's, I should say."

"What has the Colonel to do with me?" was his fierce reply, and he turned as if about to go into the house.

"Only this," I calmly answered; "I think he will get his house done first."

He wheeled and faced me, and his eye which had looked simply sullen shot a fierce and dangerous gleam.

"What makes you think that?" he cried.

"He has come back, and to-day engaged twenty extra men to push on the work."

"Indeed!" and there was contempt in his tone. "Well, I wish him joy and a sound roof!"

And this time he did go into the house.

As he had not asked me to follow, I of course had no alternative but to ride on. As I did so, I took another look at the house and saw with a strange pang at the heart that the plastering was on the walls and the windows ready for glazing. "I was wrong," said I to myself; "it is Orrin's house which will be finished first."

*   *   *   *   *

And what if it is? Will she turn her back upon the Colonel's lofty structure and take refuge in this cottage remote from the world? I cannot believe it, knowing how she loves show and the smiles and gallantries of men. And yet—and yet, she is so capricious and Orrin so determined that I do not know what to think or what to fear, and I ride back with a heavy heart, wishing she had never come up from the farm to worry and inflame the souls of honest men.

*   *   *   *   *

And now the Colonel's work goes on apace, and the whole town is filled with the noise and bustle of lumbering carts and eager workmen. The roof which Orrin so bitterly wished might be a sound one has been shingled; and under the Colonel's eye and the Colonel's constant encouragement, part after part of the new building is being fitted to its place with a precision and despatch that to many minds promise the near dawning of Juliet's wedding-day. But I know that afar in the east another home is nearer completion than this, and whether she knows it too or does not know it (which is just as probable), her wilful, sportive, and butterfly nature seems to be preparing itself for a struggle which may rend if not destroy its airy and delicate wings.

I have prepared myself too, and being still and always her friend, I stand ready to mediate or assist, as opportunity offers or circumstances demand. She realizes this, and leans on me in her secret hours of fear, or why does her face brighten when she sees me, and her little hand thrust itself confidingly forth from under its shrouding mantle and grasp mine with such a lingering and entreating pressure? And the

            Anna Katharine Green

Colonel? Does he realize, too, that I am any more to her than her other cast-off lovers and would-be friends? Sometimes I think he does, and eyes me with suspicion. But he is ever so courteous that I cannot be sure, and so do not trouble myself in regard to a jealousy so illy founded and so easily dispelled.

He is always at Juliet's side and seems to surround her with a devotion which will make it very difficult for any other man, even Orrin, to get her ear.

*　*　*　*　*

The crisis is approaching. Orrin is again in town, and may be seen riding up and down the streets in his holiday clothes. Have some whispers of his secret love and evident intentions reached the ear of the Colonel? Or is Juliet's father alone concerned? For I see that the blinds of her lattice are tightly shut, and watch as I may, I cannot catch a glimpse of her eager head peering between them at the flaunting horseman as he goes careering by.

*　*　*　*　*

The hour has come and how different is the outcome from any I had imagined. I was sitting last night in my own lonely little room, which opens directly on the street, struggling as best I might against the distraction of my thoughts which would lead me from the book I was studying, when a knock on the panels of my door aroused me, and almost before I could look up, that same door swung open and a dark form entered and stood before me.

For a moment I was too dazed to see who it was, and rising ceremoniously, I made my bow of welcome, starting a little as I met the Colonel's dark eyes looking at me from the folds of the huge mantle in which he had wrapped himself. "Your worship?" I began, and stumbling awkwardly, offered him a chair which he refused with a gesture of his smooth white hand.

"Thank you, no," said he, "I do not sit down in your house till I know if it is you who have stolen the heart of my bride away from me and if it is you with whom she is prepared to flee."

"Ah," was my involuntary exclamation, "then it has come. You know her folly, and will forgive it because she is such a child."

"Her folly? Are you not then the man?" he cried; but in a subdued tone which showed what a restraint he was putting upon himself even in the moment of such accumulated emotions.

"No," said I; "if your bride meditates flight, it is not with me she means to go. I am her friend, and the man who would take her from you is not. I can say no more, Colonel Schuyler."

He eyed me for a moment with a deep and searching gaze which showed me that his intellect was not asleep though his heart was on fire.

"I believe you," said he; and threw aside his cloak and sat down. "And now," he asked, "who is the man?"

Taken by surprise, I stammered and uttered some faint disclaimer; but seeing by his steady look and firm-set jaw that he meant to know, and detecting as I also thought in his general manner and subdued tones the promise of an unexpected forbearance, I added impulsively:

Anna Katharine Green

"Let the wayward girl tell you herself; perhaps in the telling she will grow ashamed of her caprice."

"I have asked her," was the stern reply, "and she is dumb." Then in softer tones he added: "How can I do anything for her if she will not confide in me. She has treated me most ungratefully, but I mean to be kind to her. Only I must first know if she has chosen worthily."

"Who is there of worth in town?" I asked, softened and fascinated by his manner. "There is no man equal to yourself."

"You say so," he cried, and waved his hand impatiently. Then with a deep and thrilling intensity which I feel yet, he repeated, "His name, his name? Tell me his name."

The Colonel is a man of power, accustomed to control men. I could not withstand his look or be unmoved by his tones. If he meant well to Orrin and to her, what was I that I should withhold Orrin's name. Falteringly I was about to speak it when a sudden sound struck my ears, and rising impetuously I drew him to the window, blowing out the candles as I passed them.

"Hark!" I cried, as the rush of pounding hoofs was heard on the road, and "Look!" I added, as a sudden figure swept by on the panting white horse so well known by all in that town.

"Is it he?" whispered the dark figure at my side as we both strained our eyes after Orrin's fast vanishing form.

"You have seen him," I returned; and drawing him back from the window, I closed the shutters with care, lest Orrin should be seized with a freak to return and detect me in conference with his heart's dearest enemy.

Silence and darkness were now about us, and the Colonel, as if anxious to avail himself of the surrounding gloom, caught my arm as I moved to relight the candles.

"Wait," said he; and I understood and stopped still.

And so we stood for a moment, he quiet as a carven statue and I restless but obedient to his wishes. When he stirred I carefully lit the candles, but I did not look at him till he had donned his cloak and pulled his hat well over his eyes. Then I turned, and eying him earnestly, said:

"If I have made a mistake—"

But he quickly interrupted me, averring:

"You have made no mistake. You are a good lad, Philo, and if it had been you—" He did not say what he would have done, but left the sentence incomplete and went on: "I know nothing of this Orrin Day, but what a woman wills she must have. Will you bring this fellow—he is your friend is he not?—to Juliet's house in the morning? Her father is set on her being the mistress of the new stone house and we three will have to reason with him, do you see?"

Astonished, I bowed with something like awe. Was he so great-hearted as this? Did he intend to give up his betrothed to the man whom she loved, and even to plead her cause with the father she feared? My admiration would have its vent, and I uttered some foolish words of sympathy, which he took with the stately, rather condescending grace which they perhaps merited; after which, he added again: "You will come, will you not?" and bowed kindly and retreated towards the door, while I, abashed and worshipful, followed with protestations that nothing should hinder me from doing his will, till he had passed through the doorway and vanished from my sight.

And yet I do not want to do his will or take Orrin to that house. I might have borne with sad equanimity to see her married to the Colonel, for he is far above me, but to Orrin— ah, that is a bitter outlook, and I must have been a fool to have promised aught that will help to bring it about. Still, am I not her sworn friend, and if she thinks she can be happy with him, ought I not to do my share towards making her so?

I wonder if the Colonel knows that Orrin too has been building himself a house?

I did not sleep last night, and I have not eaten this morning. Thoughts robbed me of sleep, and a visit from Orrin effectually took away from me whatever appetite I might have had. He came in almost at daybreak. He looked dishevelled and wild, and spoke like a man who had stopped more than once at the tavern.

"Philo," said he, "you have annoyed me by your curiosity for more than a year; now you can do me a favor. Will you call at Juliet's house and see if she is free to go and come as she was a week ago?"

"Why?" I asked, thinking I perceived a reason for his bloodshot eye, and yet being for the moment too wary, perhaps too ungenerous, to relieve him from the tension of his uncertainty.

"Why?" he repeated. "Must you know all that goes on in my mind, and cannot I keep one secret to myself?"

"You ask me to do you a favor," I quietly returned. "In order to do it intelligently, I must know why it is asked."

"I do not see that," objected Orrin, "and if you were not such a boy I'd leave you on the spot and do the errand myself. But you mean no harm, and so I will tell you that Juliet and I had planned to run away together last night, but though I was at the place of meeting, she did not come, nor has she made any sign to show me why she failed me."

"Orrin," I began, but he stopped me with an oath.

"No sermons," he protested. "I know what you would have done if instead of smiling on me she had chanced to give all her poor little heart to you."

"I should not have tempted her to betray the Colonel," I exclaimed hotly, perhaps because the sudden picture he presented to my imagination awoke within me such a torrent of unsuspected emotions. "Nor should I have urged her to fly with me by night and in stealth."

"You do not know what you would do," was his rude and impatient rejoinder. "Had she looked at you, with tears in her arch yet pathetic blue eyes, and listened while you poured out your soul, as if heaven were opening before her and she had no other thought in life but you, then—"

"Hush!" I cried, "do you want me to go to her house for you, or do you want me to stay away?"

"You know I want you to go."

"Then be still, and listen to what I have to say. I will go, but you must go too. If you want to take Juliet away from the Colonel you must do it openly. I will not abet you, nor will I encourage any underhanded proceedings."

"You are a courageous lad," he said, "in other men's affairs.

Will you raise me a tomb if the Colonel runs me through with his sword?"

"I at least should not feel the contempt for you which I should if you eloped with her behind his back."

"Now you are courageous on your own behalf," laughed he, "and that is better and more to the point." Yet he looked as if he could easily spit me on his own sword, which I noticed was dangling at his heels.

"Will you come?" I urged, determined not to conciliate or enlighten him even if my forbearance cost me my life.

He hesitated, and then broke into a hoarse laugh. "I have drunk just enough to be reckless," said he; "yes, I will go; and the devil must answer for the result."

I had never seen him look so little the gentleman, and perhaps it was on this very account I became suddenly quite eager to take him at his word before time and thought should give him an opportunity to become more like himself; for I could not but think that if she saw him in this condition she must make comparisons between him and the Colonel which could not but be favorable to the latter. But it was still quite early, and I dared not run the risk of displeasing the Colonel by anticipating his presence, so I urged Orrin into that little back parlor of mine, where I had once hoped to see a very different person installed, and putting wine and biscuits before him, bade him refresh himself while I prepared myself for appearing before the ladies.

When the hour came for us to go I went to him. He was pacing the floor and trying to school himself into patience, but he made but a sorry figure, and I felt a twinge of conscience as he thrust on his hat without any attempt to smooth his dishevelled locks, or rearrange his disordered ruffles. Should I permit him to go thus disordered, or should I detain him long enough to fit him for the eye of the dainty Juliet? He answered the question himself. "Come," said he, "I have chewed my sleeve long enough in suspense. Let us go and have an end of it. If she is to be my wife she must leave the house with me to-day, if not, I have an hour's work before me down yonder," and he pointed in the direction of his new house. "When you see the sky red at noonday, you will know what that is."

"Orrin!" I cried, and for the first time I seized his arm with something like a fellow-feeling.

But he shook me off.

"Don't interfere with me," he said, and strode on, sullen and fierce, towards the place where such a different greeting awaited him from any that he feared.

Ought I to tell him this? Ought I to say: "Your sullenness is uncalled for and your fierceness misplaced; Juliet is constant, and the Colonel means you nothing but good"? Perhaps; and perhaps, too, I should be a saint and know nothing of earthly passions and jealousies. But I am not. I hate this Orrin, hate him more and more as every step brings us nearer to Juliet's house and the fate awaiting him from her weakness and the Colonel's generosity. So I hold my peace and we come to her gate, and the recklessness that has brought him thus far abandons him on the instant and he falls back and lets me go in several steps before him, so that I seem to be alone when I enter the house, and Juliet, who is standing in the parlor between the Colonel and her father, starts when she sees me, and breaking into sobs, cries:

"Oh, Philo, Philo, tell my father there is nothing between us

Anna Katharine Green

but what is friendly and honorable; that I—I—"

"Hush!" commanded that father, while I stared at the Colonel, whose quiet, imperturbable face was for the first time such a riddle to me that I hardly heeded what the elder man said. "You have talked enough, Juliet, and denied enough. I will now speak to Mr. Adams and see what he has to say. Last night my daughter, who, as all the town knows, is betrothed to this gentleman"—and he waved his hand deferentially towards the Colonel—"was detected by me stealing out of the garden gate with a little packet on her arm. As my daughter never goes out alone, I was naturally startled, and presuming upon my rights as her father, naturally asked her where she was going. This question, simple as it was, seemed to both terrify and unnerve her. Stumbling back, she looked me wildly in the eye and answered, with an effrontery she had never shown me before, that she was flying to escape a hated marriage. That Colonel Schuyler had returned, and as she could not be his wife, she was going to her aunt's house, where she could live in peace without being forced upon a man she could not love. Amazed, for I had always supposed her duly sensible of the honor which had been shown her by this gentleman's attentions, I drew her into my study and there, pulling off the cloak which she held tightly drawn about her, I discovered that she was tricked out like a bride, and had a whole bunch of garden roses fastened in her breast. 'A pretty figure,' cried I, 'for travelling. You are going away with some man, and it is a runaway match I have interrupted.' She could not deny it, and just then the Colonel came in and—but we will not talk about that. It remained for us to find out the man who had led her to forget her duty, and I could think of no man but you. So I ask you now before my trembling daughter and this outraged gentleman if you are the villain."

But here Colonel Schuyler spoke up quietly and without

visible anger: "I was about to say when this gentleman's entrance interrupted my words that I had been convinced overnight that our first suspicions were false, and that Mr. Adams was, as your daughter persists in declaring, simply a somewhat zealous friend."

"But," hastily vociferated the old man, "there has been no one else about my daughter for months. If Mr. Adams is not to blame for this attempted escapade, who is? I should like to see the man, and see him standing just there."

"Then look and tell me what you think of him," came with an insolent fierceness from the doorway, and Orrin, booted and spurred, with mud on his holiday hose, and his hat still on his head, strode into our midst and confronted us all with an air of such haughty defiance that it half robbed him of his ruffianly appearance.

Juliet shrieked and stepped back, fascinated and terrified. The Colonel frowned darkly, and the old man, who had seemed by his words to summon him before us, quailed at the effect of his words and stood looking from the well-known but unexpected figure thus introduced amongst us, to the Colonel who persistently avoided his gaze, till the situation became unbearable, and I turned about as if to go.

Instantly the Colonel took advantage of the break and spoke to Orrin: "And so it is to you, sir, that I have to address the few words I have to say?"

"Yes, to him and to me!" cried little Juliet, and gliding from between the two natural protectors of her girlhood she crossed the floor and stood by Orrin's side.

This action, so unexpected and yet so natural, took away whatever restraint we had hitherto placed upon ourselves,

Anna Katharine Green

and the Colonel looked for a moment as if his self-control would abandon him entirely and leave him a prey to man's fiercest and most terrible passions. But he has a strong soul, and before I could take a step to interpose myself between him and Juliet, his face had recovered its steady aspect and his hands ceased from their ominous trembling. Her father, on the contrary, seemed to grow more ireful with every instant that he saw her thus defiant of his authority, while Orrin, pleased with her courage and touched, I have no doubt, by the loving confidence of her pleading eyes, threw his arm about her with a gesture of pride which made one forget still more his disordered and dishevelled condition.

I said nothing, but I did not leave the room.

"Juliet!"—the words came huskily from the angry father's lips, "come from that man's embrace, and do not make me shudder that I ever welcomed the Colonel to my dishonored house."

But the Colonel, putting out his hand, said calmly:

"Let her stay; since she has chosen this very honorable gentleman to be her husband, where better could she stand than by his side?"

Then forcing himself still more to seem impassive, he bowed to Orrin, and with great suavity remarked: "If she had chosen me to that honor, as I had every reason to believe she had, it would not have been many more weeks before I should have welcomed her into a home befitting her beauty and her ambition. May I ask if you can do as much for her? Have you a home for your bride in which I may look forward to paying her the respects which my humble duty to her demands?"

Ah then, Orrin towered proudly, and the pretty Juliet smiled with something of her old archness.

"Saddle your horse," cried the young lover, "and ride to the east. If you do not find a wee, fresh nest there, I am no prophet. What! steal a wife and not have a home to put her in!"

And he laughed till the huge brown rafters above his head seemed to tremble, so blithe did he feel, and so full of pride at thus daring the one great man in the town.

But the Colonel did not laugh, nor did he immediately answer. He had evidently not heard of the little cottage beyond both thicket and stream, and was consequently greatly disconcerted. But just when we were all wondering what held him so restrained, and what the words were which should break the now oppressive silence, he spoke and said:

"A wee nest is no place for the lady who was to have been my wife. If you will have patience and wait a month she shall have the home that has been reared for her. The great stone house would not know any other mistress, and therefore it shall be hers."

"No, no," Orrin began, aghast at such generosity. But the thoughtless Juliet, delighted at a prospect which promised her both splendor and love, uttered such a cry of joy that he stopped abashed and half angry, and turning upon her, said: "Are you not satisfied with what I can give you, and must you take presents even from the man you have affected to despise?"

"But, but, he is so good," babbled out the inconsiderate little thing, "and—and I do like the great stone house, and we could be so happy in it, just like a king and queen, if—if—"

She had the grace to stop, perhaps because she saw nothing but rebuke in the faces around her. But the Colonel, through whose voice ran in spite of himself an icy vein of sarcasm, observed, with another of his low bows:

"You shall indeed be like king and queen there. If you do not believe me, come there with me a month hence, and I will show you what a disappointed man can do for the woman he has loved." And taking by the arm the old man who with futile rage had tried more than once to break into this ominous conversation, he drew him persuasively to his side, and so by degrees from the room.

"Oh," cried Juliet, as the door closed behind them, "can he mean it? Can he mean it?"

And Orrin, a little awed, did not reply, but I saw by his face and bearing that whether the Colonel meant it or not was little to him; that the cottage beyond the woods was the destined home of his bride, and that we must be prepared to lose her from our midst, perhaps before the month was over which the Colonel had bidden them to wait.

I do not know through whom Dame Gossip became acquainted with yesterday's events, but everywhere in town people are laying their heads together in wonder over the jilting of Colonel Schuyler and the unprecedented magnanimity which he has shown in giving his new house to the rebellious lovers. If I have been asked one question to-day, I have been asked fifty, and Orrin, who flies into a rage at the least intimation that he will accept the gift which has been made him, spends most of his time in asserting his independence, and the firm resolution which he has made to owe nothing to the generosity of the man he has treated with such unquestionable baseness. Juliet keeps very quiet, but from the glimpse I caught of her this afternoon at her casement, I judge that the turn of affairs has had a very enlivening effect upon her beauty. Her eyes fairly sparkled as she saw me; and with something like her old joyous abandonment of manner, she tore off a branch of the flowering almond at her window and tossed it with delicious laughter at my feet. Yet though I picked it up and carried it for a few steps beyond her gate, I soon dropped it over the wall, for her sparkle and her laughter hurt me, and I would rather have seen her less joyous and a little more sensible of the ruin she had wrought.

For she has wrought ruin, as any one can see who looks at the Colonel long enough to note his eye. For though he holds himself erect and walks proudly through the town, there is that in his look which makes me tremble and hold my own weak complainings in check. He has been up to his house to-day, and when he came back there was not a blind from one end of the street to the other but quivered when he went by, so curious are the women to see him who they cannot but feel has merited all the sympathy if not the homage of their sex. Ralph Urphistone tells me to-night that the workmen at the new house have been offered extra wages if they put the house into habitable condition by the end of the month.

* * * * *

For all his secret satisfaction Orrin is very restless. He has tried to induce Juliet to marry him at once, and go with him to the little cottage he has raised for her comfort. But she puts him off with excuses, which, however, are so mingled with sweet coquetries and caresses, that he cannot reproach her without seeming insensible to her affection, and it is not until he is away from the fascination of her presence, and amongst those who do not hesitate to say that he will yet see the advantage of putting his brilliant bird in a cage suitable to her plumage, that he remembers his manhood and chafes at his inability to assert it. I am sorry for him in a way, but not so deeply as I might be if *he* were more humble and more truly sensible of the mischief he has wrought.

* * * * *

Orrin will yet make himself debtor to the Colonel. Something has happened which proves that fate—or man—is working against him to this end, and that he must from the very force of circumstances finally succumb. I say *man*, but do I not mean *woman*? Ah, no, no, no! my pen ran away with me, my thoughts played me false. It could have been no woman, for if it was, then is Juliet a—Let me keep to facts. I have not self-control enough for speculation.

To-day the sun set red. As we had been having gray skies, and more or less rain for a fortnight, the brightness and vivid crimson in the west drew many people to their doors. I was amongst them, and as I stood looking intently at the sky that was now one blaze of glory from horizon to zenith, Orrin stepped up behind me and said:

"Do you want to take a ride to-night?"

Seeing him look more restless and moody than ever, I answered "Yes," and accordingly about eight that night he rode up to my door and we started forth.

I thought he would turn in the direction of the stone house, for one night when I had allowed myself to go there in my curiosity at its progress, I had detected him crouching in one of the thickest shadows cast by the surrounding trees. But if any such idea had been in his mind, it soon vanished, for almost the instant I was in the saddle, he wheeled himself about and led the way eastward, whipping and spurring his horse as if it were a devil's ride he contemplated, and not that easy, restful canter under the rising moon demanded by our excited spirits and the calm, exquisite beauty of the summer night.

"Are you not coming?" was shouted back to me, as the distance increased between us.

My answer was to spur my own horse, and as we rode once more side by side, I could not but note what a wild sort of beauty there was in him as he thus gave himself up to the force of his feelings and the restless energy of this harum-scarum ride. "Very different," thought I, "would the Colonel look on a horse at this hour of night"; and wondered if Juliet could see him thus she would any longer wound him by her hesitations, after having driven him by her coquetries to expect full and absolute surrender on her part.

Did he guess my thoughts, or was his mind busy with the same, that he suddenly cried in harsh but thrilling tones:

"If I had her where she ought to be, here behind me on this horse, I would ride to destruction before I would take her back again to the town and the temptations which beset her while she can hear the sound of hammer upon stone."

"And you would be right," I was about to say in some bitterness, I own, when the full realization of the road we were upon stopped me and I observed instead:

"You would take her yonder where you hope to see her happy, though no other woman lives within a half-mile of the place."

"No man you should say," quoth Orrin bitterly, lashing his horse till it shot far ahead of me, so that some few minutes passed before we were near enough together for him to speak again. Then he said: "She loads me with promises and swears that she loves me more than all the world. If half of this is true she ought to be happy with me in a hovel, while I have a dainty cottage for her dwelling, where the vines will soon grow and the birds sing. You have not seen it since it has been finished. You shall see it to-night."

I choked as I tried to answer, and wondered if he had any idea of what I had to contend with in these rides I seemed forced to take without any benefit to myself. If he had, he was merciless, for once launched into talk he kept on till I was almost wild with hateful sympathy and jealous chagrin. Suddenly he paused.

The forest we had been threading had for the last few minutes been growing thinner, and as the quick cessation in his speech caused me to look up, I saw, or thought I saw, a faint glow shining through the branches before me, which could not have come from the reflection made by the setting sun, as that had long ago sunk into darkness.

Orrin who, as he had ceased speaking, had suddenly reined in his panting horse, now gave a shout and shot forward, and I, hardly knowing what to fear or expect, followed him as fast as my evidently weary animal would carry me, and thus bounding along with but a few paces between us, we cleared the woods and came out into the open fields beyond. As we did so a cry went up from Orrin, faintly echoed by my own lips. It was a fire that we saw, and the flames, which had now got furious headway, rose up like pillars to the sky, illuminating all the country round, and showing me, both by their position and the glare of the stream beneath them, that it was Orrin's house which was burning, and Orrin's hopes which were being destroyed before our eyes. The cry he gave as he fully realized this I shall never forget, nor the gesture with which he drove his spurs into his horse and flashed down that long valley into the ever-increasing glare that lighted first his flowing hair and the wet flanks of the animal he bestrode, and finally seemed to envelop him altogether, till he looked like some avenging demon rushing through his own element of fury and fire.

I was far behind him, but I made what time I could, feeling to the core, as I passed, the weirdness of the solitude before me, with just this element of horror flaming up in its midst. Not a sound save that of our pounding hoofs interrupted that crackling sound of burning wood, and when the roof fell in, as it did before I could reach his side, I could hear distinctly the echo which followed it. Orrin may have heard it too, for he gave a groan and drew in his horse, and when I reached him I saw him sitting there before the smouldering ashes of his home, silent and inert, without a word to say or an ear to hear the instinctive words of sympathy I could not now keep back.

Who had done it? Who had started the blaze which had in one half-hour undone the work and hope of months? That was the question which first roused me and caused me to search the silence and darkness of the night for some trace of a human presence, if only so much as the mark of a human foot. And I found it. There, in the wet margin of the stream, I came upon a token which may mean nothing and which may mean—But I cannot write even here of the doubts it brought me; I will only tell how on our slow and wearisome passage home through the sombre woods, Orrin suddenly let his bridle fall, and, flinging up his arms above his head, cried bitterly:

"O that I did not love her so well! O that I had never seen her who would make of me a slave when I would be a man!"

*　*　*　*　*

The gossips at the corners nod knowingly this morning, and Orrin, whose brow is moodier than the Colonel's, walks fiercely amongst them without word and without look. He is on his way to Juliet's house, and if there is enchantment left in smiles, I bid her to use it, for her fate is trembling in the balance, and may tip in a direction of which she little recks.

* * * * *

Orrin has come back. Striding impetuously into the room where I sat at work, he drew himself up till his figure showed itself in all its full and graceful proportions.

"Am I a man?" he asked, "or," with a fall in his voice brimmed with feeling, "am I a fool? She met me with such an unsuspicious look, Philo, and bore herself with such an innocent air, that I not only could not say what I meant to say, but have promised to do what I have sworn never to do—accept the Colonel's unwelcome gift, and make her mistress of the new stone house."

"You are—a man," I answered. For what are men but fools where women of such enchantment are concerned!

He groaned, perhaps at the secret sarcasm hidden in my tone, and sat down unbidden at the table where I was writing.

"You did not see her," he cried. "You do not know with what charms she works, when she wishes to comfort and allure." Ah! did I not. "And Philo," he went on, almost humbly for him, "you are mistaken if you think she had any hand in the ruin which has come upon me. She had not. How I know it I cannot say, but I am ready to swear it, and you must forget any foolish fears I may have shown or any foolish words I may have uttered in the first confusion of my loss and disappointment."

"I will forget," said I.

"The fact is I do not understand her," he eagerly explained. "There was innocence in her air, but there was mockery too, and she laughed as I talked of my grief and rage, as though she thought I was playing a part. It was merry laughter, and there was no ring of falsehood in it, but why should she laugh at all?"

This was a question I could not answer; who could? Juliet is beyond the comprehension of us all.

"But what is the use of plaguing myself with riddles?" he now asked, starting up as suddenly as he had sat down. "We are to be married in a month, and the Colonel—I have seen the Colonel—has promised to dance at our wedding. Will it be in the new stone house? It would be a fitting end to this comedy if he were to dance in *that*?"

I thought as Orrin did about this, but with more seriousness perhaps; and it was not till after he had left me that I remembered I had not asked whom he suspected of firing his house, now that he was assured of the innocence of her who was most likely to profit by its burning.

*   *   *   *   *

"Now I understand Juliet!" was the cry with which Orrin burst into my presence late this afternoon. "Men are saying and women whispering that I destroyed my own house, in order to save myself the shame of accepting the Colonel's offer while I had a roof of my own." And, burning with rage, he stamped his foot upon the ground, and shook his hand so threateningly in the direction of his fancied enemies that I felt some reflection of his anger in my own breast, and said or tried to say that they could not know him as I did or they would never accuse him of so mean a deed, whatever else they might bring against him.

"It makes me wild, it makes me mad, it makes me feel like leaving the town forever!" was his hoarse complaint as I finished my feeble attempt at consolation. "If Juliet were half the woman she ought to be she would come and live with me in a log-cabin in the woods before she would accept the Colonel's house now. And to think that she, *she* should be affected by the opinions of the rest, and think me so destitute of pride that I would stoop to sacrifice my own home for the sake of stepping into that of a rival's. O woman, woman, what are you made of? Not of the same stuff as we men, surely."

I strove to calm him, for he was striding fiercely and impatiently about the room. But at my first word he burst forth with:

"And her father, who should control her, aids and encourages her follies. He is a slave to the Colonel, who is the slave of his own will."

"In this case," I quietly observed, "his will seems to be most kindly."

"That is the worst of it," chafed Orrin. "If only he offered me opposition I could struggle with him. But it is his generosity I hate, and the humiliating position into which it thrusts me. And that is not all," he angrily added, while still striding feverishly about the room. "The Colonel seems to think us his property ever since we decided to accept his, and as a miser watches over his gold so does he watch over us, till I scarcely have the opportunity now of speaking to Juliet alone. If I go to her house, there he is sitting like a black statue at the fireplace, and when I would protest, and lead her into another room or into the garden, he rises and over-whelms me with such courtesies and subtle disquisitions that I am tripped up in my endeavors, and do not know how to leave or how to stay. I wish he would fall sick, or his house tumble about his head!"

"Orrin, Orrin!" I cried. But he interrupted my remonstrance with the words:

"It is not decent. I am her affianced husband now, and he should leave us alone. Does he think I can ever forget that he used to court her once himself, and that the favors she now shows me were once given as freely, if not as honestly, to him? He knows I cannot forget, and he delights—"

"There, Orrin," I broke in, "you do him wrong. The Colonel is above your comprehension as he is above mine; but there is nothing malevolent in him."

"I don't know about that," rejoined his angry rival. "If he wanted to steal back my bride he could take no surer course for doing it. Juliet, who is fickle as the wind, already looks from his face to mine as if she were contrasting us. And he is so damned handsome and suave and self-forgetting!"

"And you," I could not help but say, "are so fierce and sullen even in your love."

"I know it," was his half-muttered retort, "but what can you expect? Do you think I will see him steal her heart away from before my eyes?"

"It would be but a natural return on his part for your former courtesies," I could not forbear saying, in my own secret chagrin and soreness of heart.

"But he shall not do it," exclaimed Orrin, with a backward toss of his head, and a sudden thump of his strong hand on the table before me. "I won her once against all odds, and I will keep her if I have to don the devil's smiles myself. He shall never again see her eyes rest longer on his face than mine. I will hold her by the power of my love till he finds himself forgotten, and for very shame steals away, leaving me with the bride he has himself bestowed upon me. He shall never have Juliet back."

"I doubt if he wishes to," I quietly remarked, as Orrin, weary with passion, ran from my presence.

I do not know whether Orrin succeeded or not in his attempts to shame the Colonel from intruding upon his interviews with Juliet. I am only sure that Orrin's countenance smoothed itself after this day, and that I heard no more complaints of Juliet's wavering fidelity. I myself do not believe she has ever wavered. Simply because she ought from every stand-point of good judgment and taste to have preferred the Colonel and clung to him, she will continue to cleave to Orrin and make him the idol of her wayward heart. But it is all a mystery to me and one that does not make me very happy.

*　*　*　*　*

I went up by myself to the new stone house to-day, and found that it only needs the finishing touches. Twenty workmen or more were there, and the great front door had just been brought and was leaning against the walls preparatory to being hung. Being curious to see how they were progressing within, I climbed up to one of the windows and looked in, and not satisfied with what I could thus see, made my way into the house and up the main staircase, which I was surprised to see was nearly completed.

The sound of the hammer and saw was all about me, and the calling of orders from above and below interfered much with any sentimental feelings I might have had. But I was not there to indulge in sentiment, and so I roamed on from room to room till I suddenly came upon a sight that drove every consideration of time and place from my mind, and made me for a moment forgetful of every other sentiment than admiration. This was nothing less than the glimpse which I obtained in passing one of the windows, of the Colonel himself down on his knees on the scaffolding aiding the workmen. So, so, he is not content with hurrying the work forward by his means and influence, but is lending the force of his example, and actually handling the plane and saw in his anxiety not to disappoint Juliet in regard to the day she has fixed for her marriage.

A week ago I should have told Orrin what I had seen, but I had no desire to behold the old frowns come back to his face, so I determined to hold my silence with him. But Juliet ought to know with what manner of heart she has been so recklessly playing, so after stealing down the stairs I felt I should never have mounted, I crept from the house and made my way as best I could through the huge forest-trees that so thickly clustered at its back, till I came upon the high-road which leads to the village. Walking straight to Juliet's house I asked to see her, and shall never forget the blooming beauty of her presence as she stepped into the room and gave me her soft white hand to kiss.

As she is no longer the object of my worship and hardly the friend of my heart, I think I can speak of her loveliness now without being misunderstood. So I will let my pen trace for once a record of her charms, which in that hour were surely great enough to excuse the rivalry of which they had been the subject, and perhaps to account for the disinterestedness of the man who had once given her his heart.

Anna Katharine Green

She is of medium height, this Juliet, and her form has that sway in it which you see in a lily nodding on its stem. But she is no lily in her most enchanting movements, but rather an ardent passion-flower burning and palpitating in the sun. Her skin, which is milk-white, has strange flushes in it, and her eyes, which never look at you twice with the same meaning, are blue, or gray, or black, as her feeling varies and the soul informing them is in a state of joy, or trouble. Her most bewitching feature is her mouth, which has two dangerous dimples near it that go and come, sometimes without her volition and sometimes, I fear, with her full accord and desire. Her hair is brown and falls in such a mass of ringlets that no cap has ever yet been found which can confine it and keep it from weaving a golden net in which to entangle the hearts of men. When she smiles you feel like rushing forward; when she frowns you question yourself humbly what you have done to merit a look so out of keeping with the playful cast of her countenance and the arch bearing of her spirited young form. She was dressed, as she always is, simply, but there was infinite coquetry in the tie of the blue ribbon on her shoulder, and if a close cap of dainty lace could make a face look more entrancing, I should like the privilege of seeing it. She was in an amiable mood and smiled upon my homage like a fairy queen.

"I have come to pay my final respects to Juliet Playfair," I announced; "for by the tokens up yonder she will soon be classed among our matrons."

My tone was formal and she looked surprised at it, but my news was welcome and so she made me a demure little courtesy before saying joyously:

"Yes, the house is nearly done, and to-morrow Orrin and I are going up there together to see it. The Colonel has asked us to do this that we might say whether all is to our liking and convenience."

"The Colonel is a man in a thousand," I began, but, seeing her frown in her old pettish way, I perceived that she partook enough of Orrin's spirit to dislike any allusion to one whose generosity threw her own selfishness into startling relief.

So I said no more on this topic, but let my courtesy expend itself in good wishes, and came away at last with a bewildering remembrance of her beauty, which I am doing my best to blot out by faithfully recounting to myself the story of those infinite caprices of hers which have come so near wrecking more than one honorable heart.

I do not expect to visit her again until I pay my respects to her as Orrin's wife.

*   *   *   *   *

It is the day when Orrin and Juliet are to visit the new house. If I had not known this from her own lips, I should have known it from the fact that the workmen all left at noon, in order, as one of them said, to leave the little lady more at her ease. I saw them coming down the road, and had the curiosity to watch for the appearance of Orrin and the Colonel at Juliet's gate but they did not come, and assured by this that they meditated a later visit than I had anticipated, I went about my work. This took me up the road, and as it chanced, led me within a few rods of the wood within which lies the new stone house. I had not meant to go there, for I have haunted the place enough, but this time there was reason for it, and satisfied with the fact, I endeavored to fix my mind on other matters and forget who was likely at any moment to enter the forest behind me.

But when one makes an effort to forget he is sure to

remember all the more keenly, and I was just picturing to my mind Juliet's face and Juliet's pretty air of mingled pride and disdain as the first sight of the broad stone front burst upon her, when I heard through the stillness of the woods the faint sound of a saw, which coming from the direction of the house seemed to say that some one was still at work there. As I had understood that all the men had been given a half-holiday, I felt somewhat surprised at this, and unconsciously to myself moved a few steps nearer the opening where the house stood, when suddenly all was still and I could not for the moment determine whether I had really heard the sound of a saw or not. Annoyed at myself, and ashamed of an interest that made every trivial incident connected with this affair of such moment to me, I turned back to my work, and in a few moments had finished it and left the wood, when what was my astonishment to see Orrin coming from the same place, with his face turned toward the village, and a hardy, determined expression upon it which made me first wonder and then ask myself if I really comprehended this man or knew what he cherished in his heart of hearts.

Going straight up to him, I said:

"Well, Orrin, what's this? Coming away from the house instead of going to it? I understood that you and Juliet were expecting to visit it together this afternoon."

He paused, startled, and his eyes fell as I looked him straight in the face.

"We are going to visit it," he admitted, "but I thought it would be wiser for me to inspect the place first and see if all was right. An unfinished building has so many traps in it, you know." And he laughed loudly and long, but his mirth was forced, and I turned and looked after him, as he strode away, with a vague but uneasy feeling I did not myself understand.

"Will the Colonel go with you?" I called out.

He wheeled about as if stung. "Yes," he shouted, "the Colonel will go with us. Did you suppose he would allow us the satisfaction of going alone? I tell you, Philo," and he strode back to my side, "the Colonel considers us his property. Is not that pleasant? His *property*! And so we are," he fiercely added, "while we are his debtors. But we shall not be his debtors long. When we are married—if we *are* married—I will take Juliet from this place if I have to carry her away by force. She shall never be the mistress of this house."

"Orrin! Orrin!" I protested.

"I have said it," was his fierce rejoinder, and he left me for the second time and passed hurriedly down the street.

I was therefore somewhat taken aback when a little while later he reappeared with Juliet and the Colonel, in such a mood of forced gayety that more than one turned to look after them as they passed merrily laughing down the road. Will Juliet never be the mistress of that house? I think she will, my Orrin. That dimpled smile of hers has more force in it than that dominating will of yours. If she chooses to hold her own she will hold it, and neither you nor the Colonel can ever say her nay.

What did Orrin tell me? That she would never be mistress of that house? Orrin was right, she never will; but who could have thought of a tragedy like this? Not I, not I; and if Orrin did and planned it—But let me tell the whole just as it happened, keeping down my horror till the last word is written and I have plainly before me the awful occurrences of this fearful day.

They went, the three, to that fatal house together, and no man, saving myself perhaps, thought much more about the matter till we began to see Juliet's father peering anxiously from over his gate in the direction of the wood. Then we realized that the afternoon had long passed and that it was getting dark; and going up to the old man, I asked whom he was looking for. The answer was as we expected.

"I am looking for Juliet. The Colonel took her and Orrin up to their new house, but they do not come back. I had a dreadful dream last night, and it frightens me. Why don't they come? It must be dark enough in the wood."

"They will come soon," I assured him, and moved off, for I do not like Juliet's father.

But when I passed by there again a half-hour later and found the old man still standing bare-headed and with craning neck at his post, I became very uneasy myself, and proposed to two or three neighbors, whom I found standing about, that we should go toward the woods and see if all were well. They agreed, being affected, doubtless, like myself, by the old man's fears, and as we proceeded down the street, others joined us till we amounted in number to a half-dozen or more. Yet, though the occasion seemed a strange one, we were not really alarmed till we found ourselves at the woods and realized how dark they were and how still. Then I began to feel an oppression at my heart, and trod with careful and hesitating steps till we came into the open space in which the house stands. Here it was lighter, but oh! how still. I shall never forget how still; when suddenly a shrill cry broke from one amongst us, and I saw Ralph Urphistone pointing with finger frozen in horror at something which lay in ghastly outline upon the broad stone which leads up to the gap of the great front door.

What was it? We dared not approach to see, yet we dared not linger quiescent. One by one we started forward till finally we all stood in a horrified circle about the thing that looked like a shadow, and yet was not a shadow, but some horrible nightmare that made us gasp and shudder till the moon came suddenly out, and we saw that what we feared and shrank from were the bodies of Juliet and Orrin, he lying with face upturned and arms thrown out, and she with her head pillowed on his breast as if cast there in her last faint moment of consciousness. They were both dead, having fallen through the planks of the scaffolding, as was shown by the fatal gap open to the moonlight above our heads. Dead! dead! and though no man there knew how, the terror of their doom and the retribution it seemed to bespeak went home to our hearts, and we bowed our heads with a simultaneous cry of terror, which in that first moment was too overwhelming even for grief.

The Colonel was nowhere to be seen, and after the first few minutes of benumbing horror, we tried to call aloud his name. But the cries died in our throat, and presently one amongst us withdrew into the house to search, and then another and another, till I was left alone in awful attendance upon the dead. Then I began to realize my own anguish, and with some last fragment of secret jealousy—or was it from some other less definite but equally imperative feeling?—was about to stoop forward and lift her head from a pillow that I somehow felt defiled it, when a quick hand drew me aside, and looking up, I saw Ralph standing at my back. He did not speak, and his figure looked ghostly in the moonlight, but his hand was pointing toward the house, and when I moved to follow him, he led the way into the hollow entrance and up the stairway till we came to the upper story where he stopped, and motioned me toward a door opening into one of the rooms.

There were several of our number already standing there, so I did not hesitate to approach, and as I went the darkness in which I had hitherto moved disappeared before the broad band of moonlight shining into the room before us, and I saw, darkly silhouetted against a shining background, the crouching figure of the Colonel, staring with hollow eyes and maddened mien out of the unfinished window through which in all probability the devoted couple had stepped to their destruction.

"Can you make him speak?" asked one. "He does not seem to heed us, though we have shouted to him and even shook his arm."

"I shall not try," said I. "Horror like this should be respected." And going softly in I took up my station by his side in silent awe.

But they would have me talk, and finally in some desperation I turned to him and said, quietly:

"The scaffolding broke beneath them, did it not?" At which he first stared and then flung up his arms with a wild but suppressed cry. But he said nothing, and next moment had settled again into his old attitude of silent horror and amazement.

"He might better be lying with them," I whispered after a moment, coming from his side. And one by one they echoed my words, and as he failed to move or even show any symptoms of active life, we gradually drifted from the spot till we were all huddled again below in the hollow blackness of that doorway guarded over by the dead.

Who should tell her father? They all looked at me, but I shook my head, and it fell to another to perform this piteous errand, for fearful thoughts were filling my brain, and Orrin did not look altogether guiltless to me as he lay there dead beside the maiden he had declared so fiercely should never be mistress of this house.

* * * * *

Was ever such a night of horror known in this town!

They have brought the two bruised bodies down into the village and they now lie side by side in the parlor where I last saw Juliet in the bloom and glow of life. The Colonel is still crouching where I left him. No one can make him speak and no one can make him move, and the terror which his terror has produced affects the whole community, not even the darkness of the night serving to lessen the wild excitement which drives men and women about the streets as if it were broad daylight, and makes of every house an open thorough-fare through which anybody who wishes can pass.

I, who have followed every change and turn in this whole calamitous affair, am like one benumbed at this awful crisis. I too go and come through the streets, hear people say in shouts, in cries, with bitter tears and wild lamentations, "Juliet is dead!" "Orrin is dead!" and get no sense from the words. I have even been more than once to that spot where they lie in immovable beauty, and though I gaze and gaze upon them, I feel nothing—not even wonder. Only the remembrance of that rigid figure frozen into its place above the gulf where so much youth and so many high hopes fell, has power to move me. When amid the shadows which surround me I see *that*, I shudder and the groan rises slowly to my lips as if I too were looking down into a gulf from which hope and love would never again rise.

*   *   *   *   *

The Colonel is now in his father's house. He was induced to leave the place by Ralph Urphistone's little child. When the great man first felt the touch of those baby fingers upon his, he shuddered and half recoiled, but as the little one pulled him gently but persistently towards the stair, he gradually yielded to her persuasion, and followed till he had descended to the ground-floor and left the fatal house. I do not think any other power could have induced him to pass that blood-stained threshold. For he seems thoroughly broken down, and will, I fear, never be the same man that he was before this fearful tragedy took place before his eyes.

All day I have paced the floor of my room asking myself if I should allow Juliet to be laid away in the same tomb as Orrin. He was her murderer, without doubt, and though he has shared her doom, was it right for me to allow one stone to be raised above their united graves. Feeling said no, but reason bade me halt before I disturbed the whole community with whispers of a crime. I therefore remained undecided, and it was in this same condition of doubt that I finally went to the funeral and stood with the rest of the lads beside the open grave which had been dug for the unhappy lovers in that sunny spot beside the great church door. At sight of this grave and the twin coffins about to be lowered into it, I felt my struggle renewed, and yet I held my peace and listened as best I could to the minister's words and the broken sobs of such as had envied these two in their days of joyance, but had only pity for pleasure so soon over and hopes doomed to such early destruction.

We were all there; Ralph and Lemuel and the other neighbors, old and young, all except that chief of mourners, the Colonel; for he was still under the influence of that horror which kept him enchained in silence, and had not even been sensible enough of the day and its mournful occasion to rise and go to the window as the long funeral cortege passed his house. We were all there and the minister had said the words, and Orrin's body had been lowered to its final rest, when suddenly, as they were about to move Juliet, a tumult was observed in the outskirts of the crowd, and the Colonel towering in his rage and appalling in his just indignation, fought his way through the recoiling masses till he stood in our very midst.

"Stop!" he cried, "this burial must not go on." And he advanced his arm above Juliet's body as if he would intervene his very heart between it and the place of darkness into which it was about to descend. "She was the victim, he the murderer; they shall not lie together if I have to fling myself between them in the grave which you have dug."

"But—but," interposed the minister, calm and composed even in the face of this portentous figure and the appalling words which it had uttered, "by what right do you call this one a murderer and the other a victim? Did you see him murder her? Was there a crime enacted before your eyes?"

"The boards were sawn," was the startling answer. "They must have been sawn or they would never have given way beneath so light a weight. And then he urged her—I saw him—pleaded with her, drew her by force of eye and hand to step upon the scaffold without, though there was no need for it, and she recoiled. And when her light foot was on it and her half-smiling, half-timid face looked back upon us, he leaped out beside her, when instantly came the sound of a great crack, and I heard his laugh and her cry go up together, and—and—everything has been midnight in my soul ever since, till suddenly through the blank and horror surrounding me I caught the words, 'They will lie together in one tomb!' Then—then I awoke and my voice came back to me and my memory, and hither I hastened to stop this unhallowed work; for to lay the victim beside her murderer is a sacrilege which I for one would come back even from the grave to prevent."

"But why," moaned the father feebly amid the cries and confusion which had been aroused by so gruesome an interference on the brink of the grave, "but why should Orrin wish my Juliet's death? They were to have been married soon—"

But piteous as were his tones no one listened, for just then a lad who had been hiding behind the throng stepped out before us, showing a face so white and a manner so perturbed that we all saw that he had something to say of importance in this matter.

"The boards *have* been sawn," he said. "I wanted to know and I climbed up to see." At which words the whole crowd moved and swayed, and a dozen hands stooped to lift the body of Juliet and carry it away from that accursed spot.

But the minister is a just man and cautious, and he lifted up his arms in such protest that they paused.

"Who knows," he suggested, "that it was Orrin's hand which handled the saw?"

And then I perceived that it was time for me to speak. So I raised my voice and told my story, and as I told it the wonder grew on every face and the head of each man slowly drooped till we all stood with downcast eyes. For crime had never before been amongst us or soiled the honor of our goodly town. Only the Colonel still stood erect; and as the vision of his outstretched arm and flaming eyes burned deeper and deeper into my consciousness, I stammered in my speech and then sobbed, and was the first to lift the silent form of the beauteous dead and bear it away from the spot denounced by one who had done so much for her happiness and had met with such a bitter and heart-breaking reward.

And where did we finally lay her? In that spot—ah! why does my blood run chill while I write it—where she stood when she took that oath to the Colonel, whose breaking caused her death.

A few words more and this record must be closed forever. That night, when all was again quiet in the village and the mourners no longer went about the streets, Lemuel, Ralph, and I went for a final visit to the new stone house. It showed no change, that house, and save for the broken scaffolding above gave no token of its having been the scene of such a woful tragedy. But as we looked upon it from across its gruesome threshold Lemuel said:

"It is a goodly structure and nigh completed, but the hand that began it will never finish it, nor will man or woman ever sleep within its walls. The place is accursed, and will stand accursed till it is consumed by God's lightning or falls piecemeal to the ground from natural decay. Though its stones are fresh, I see ruin already written upon its walls."

It was a strong statement, and we did not believe it, but when we got back to the village we were met by one who said:

"The Colonel has stopped the building of the new house. 'It is to be an everlasting monument,' he says, 'to a rude man's pride and a sweet woman's folly.'"

Will it be a monument that he will love to gaze upon? I wot not, or any other man who remembers Juliet's loveliness and the charm it gave to our village life for one short year.

Anna Katharine Green

*   *   *   *   *

What was it that I said about this record being at an end? Some records do not come to an end, and though twenty years have passed since I wrote the above, I have cause this day to take these faded leaves from their place and add a few lines to the story of the Colonel's new house.

It is an old house now, old and desolate. As Lemuel said—he is one of our first men—it is accursed and no one has ever felt brave enough or reckless enough to care to cross again its ghostly threshold. Though I never heard any one say it is haunted, there are haunting memories enough surrounding it for one to feel a ghastly recoil from invading precincts defiled by such a crime. So the kindly forest has taken it into its protection, and Nature, who ever acts the generous part, has tried to throw the mantle of her foliage over the decaying roof, and about the lonesome walls, accepting what man forsakes and so fulfilling her motherhood.

I am still a resident in the town, and I have a family now that has outgrown the little cottage which the apple-tree once guarded. But it is not to tell of them or of myself that I have taken these pages from their safe retreat to-day, but to speak of the sight which I saw this morning when I passed through the churchyard, as I often do, to pluck a rose from the bush which we lads planted on Juliet's grave twenty years ago. They always seem sweeter to me than other roses, and I take a superstitious delight in them, in which my wife, strange to say, does not participate. But that is neither here nor there.

The sight which I thought worth recording was this: I had come slowly through the yard, for the sunshine was brilliant and the month June, and sad as the spot is, it is strangely beautiful to one who loves nature, when as I approached the corner where Juliet lies, and which you will remember was in the very spot where I once heard her take her reluctant oath, I saw crouched against her tomb a figure which seemed both strange and vaguely familiar to me. Not being able to guess who it was, as there is now nobody in town who remembers her with any more devotion than myself, I advanced with sudden briskness, when the person I was gazing upon rose, and turning towards me, looked with deeply searching and most certainly very wretched eyes into mine. I felt a shock, first of surprise, and then of wildest recollection. The man before me was the Colonel, and the grief apparent in his face and disordered mien showed that years of absence had not done their work, and that he had never forgotten the arch and brilliant Juliet.

Bowing humbly and with a most reverent obeisance, for he was still the great man of the county, though he had not been in our town for years, I asked his pardon for my intrusion, and then drew back to let him pass. But he stopped and gave me a keen look, and speaking my name, said: "You are married, are you not?" And when I bowed the meek acquiescence which the subject seemed to demand, he sighed as I thought somewhat bitterly, and shrugging his shoulders, went thoughtfully by and left me standing on the green sward alone. But when he had reached the gate he turned again, and without raising his voice, though the distance between us was considerable, remarked: "I have come back to spend my remaining days in the village of my birth. If you care to talk of old times, come to the house at sunset. You will find me sitting on the porch."

Gratified more than I ever expected to be by a word from him, I bowed my thanks and promised most heartily to come. And that was the end of our first interview.

It has left me with very lively sensations. Will they be increased or diminished by the talk he has promised me?

*   *   *   *   *

I had a pleasant hour with the Colonel, but we did not talk of *her*. Had I expected to? I judge so by the faint but positive disappointment which I feel.

*   *   *   *   *

I have been again to the Colonel's, but this time I did not find him in. "He is much out evenings," explained the woman who keeps house for him, "and you will have to come early to see him at his own hearth."

*   *   *   *   *

What is there about the Colonel that daunts me? He seems friendly, welcomes my company, and often hands me the hospitable glass. But I am never easy in his presence, though the distance between us is not so great as it was in our young days, now that I have advanced in worldly prosperity and he has stood still. Is it that his intellect cows me, or do I feel too much the secret melancholy which breathes through all his actions, and frequently cuts short his words? I cannot answer; I am daunted by him and I am fascinated, and after leaving him think only of the time when I shall see him again.

*   *   *   *   *

The children, who have grown up since the Colonel has been gone, seem very shy of him. I have noted them more than once shrink away from his path, huddling and whispering in a corner, and quite forgetting to play as long as his shadow fell across the green or the sound of his feet could be heard on the turf. I think they fear his melancholy, not understanding it. Or perhaps some hint of his sorrows has been given them, and it is awe they feel rather than fear. However that may be, no child ever takes his hand or prattles to him of its little joys or griefs; and this in itself makes him look solitary, for we are much given in this town to merry-making with our little ones, and it is a common sight to see old and young together on the green, making sport with ball or battledore.

And it is not the children only who hold him in high but distant respect. The best men here are contented with a courteous bow from him, while the women—matrons now, who once were blushing maidens—think they have shown him enough honor if they make him a deep curtsey and utter a mild "Good-morrow."

The truth is, he invites nothing more. He talks to me because he must talk to some one, but our conversation is always of things outside of our village life, and never by any chance of the place or any one in it. He lives at his father's house, now his, and has for his sole companion an old servant of the family, who was once his nurse, and who is, I believe, the only person in the world who is devotedly attached to him.

Unless it is myself. Sometimes I think I love him; sometimes I think I do not. He fascinates me, and could make me do most anything he pleased, but have I a real affection for him? Almost; and this is something which I consider strange.

* * * * *

Where does the Colonel go evenings? His old nurse has asked me, and I find I cannot answer. Not to the tavern, for I am often there; not to the houses of the neighbors, for none of them profess to know him. Where then? Is the curiosity of my youth coming back to me? It looks very much like it, Philo, very much like it.

Anna Katharine Green

*　*　*　*　*

My daughter said to me to-day: "Father, do not go any more to the Colonel's." And when I asked her why, she answered that her lover—she has a *lover*, the minx—had told her that the Colonel held secret talks with the witches, and though I laughed at this, it has set me thinking. He goes to the forest at night, and roams for hours among its shadows. Is this a healthy occupation for a man, especially a man with a history? I shall go early to the Schuyler homestead to-night and stay late, for these midnight communings with nature may be the source of the hideous gloom which I have observed of late is growing upon his spirits. No other duty seems to me now greater than this, to win him back to a healthy realization of life, and the need there is of looking cheerfully upon such blessings as are left to our lot.

*　*　*　*　*

I went to the Colonel's at early candle-light, and I stayed till ten, a late hour for me, and, as I hoped, for him. When I left I caught a sight of old Hannah, standing in a distant hallway, and I thought she looked grateful; at all events, she came forward very quickly after my departure, for I heard the key turn in the lock of the great front door before I had passed out of the gate.

Why did I not go home? I had meant to, and there was every reason why I should. But I had no sooner felt the turf under my feet and seen the stars over my head, than I began to wander in the very opposite direction, and that without any very definite plan or purpose. I think I was troubled, and if not troubled, restless, and yet movement did not seem to help me, for I grew more uneasy with every step I took, and began to look towards the woods to which I was half unconsciously tending as if there I should find relief just as the Colonel, perhaps, was in the habit of doing. Was it a mere foolish freak which had assailed me, or was I under some uncanny influence, caught from the place where I had been visiting?

I was yet asking myself this, when I heard distinctly through the silence of the night the sound of a footstep behind me, and astonished that any one else should have been beguiled at this hour into a walk so dreary, I slipped into the shadow of a tree that stood at the wayside and waited till the slowly advancing figure should pass and leave me free to pursue my way or to go back unnoticed and undisturbed.

I had not long to wait. In a moment a weirdly muffled form appeared abreast of me, and it was with difficulty I suppressed a cry, for it was the Colonel I saw, escaped, doubtless, from his old nurse's surveillance, and as he passed he groaned, and the sad sound coming through the night at a time when my own spirits were in no comfortable mood affected me with almost a superstitious power, so that I trembled where I stood and knew not whether to follow him or go back and seek the cheer of my own hearth. But I decided in another moment to follow him, and when he had withdrawn far enough up the road not to hear the sound of my footfalls, I stepped out from my retreat and went with him into the woods.

I have been as you know a midnight wanderer in that same place many a time in my life; but never did I leave the fields and meadows with such a foreboding dread, or step into the clustering shadows of the forest with such a shrinking and awe-struck heart. Yet I went on without a pause or an instant of hesitation, for I knew now where he was going, and if he were going to the old stone house I was determined to be his companion, or at least his watcher. For I knew now that I loved him and could never see him come to ill.

There was no moon at this time, but the sound of his steps guided me and when I had come into the open place where the stars shone I saw by the movement which took place in the shadows lying around the open door of the old house, that he was near the fatal threshold and would in another moment be across it and within those mouldy halls. That I was right, another instant proved, for suddenly through the great hollow of the open portal a mild gleam broke and I saw he had lighted a lantern and was moving about within the empty rooms.

Softly as man could go, I followed him. Crouching in the doorway, with ear turned to the emptiness within, I listened. And as I did so, I felt the chill run through my blood and stiffen the hair on my head, for he was talking as he walked, and his tones were affable and persuasive, as if two ghosts roamed noiselessly at his side and he were showing them as in the days of yore, the beauties of his nearly completed home.

"An ample parlor, you see," came in distinct, suave mono-tone to my ear. "Room enough for many a couple on gala nights, as even sweet Mistress Juliet will say. Do you like this fireplace, and will there be space enough here for the portrait which Lawrence has promised to make of young Madam Day? I do not like too much light myself, so I have ordered curtains to be hung here. But if Mistress Juliet prefers the sunshine, we will tell the men nay, for all is to be according to your will, fair lady, as you must know, being here. Pardon me, that was an evil step; you should have a quick eye for such mishaps, friend Orrin, and not leave it to my courtesy to hold out a helping hand. Ah! you like this dusky nook. It was made for a sweet young bride to hide in when her heart's fulness demands quiet and rest. Do the trees come too near the lattice? If so they shall be trimmed away. And this dining-parlor—Can you judge of it with the floor half laid and its wainscoting unnailed? I trow not, but you can trust me, pretty Juliet, you can trust me; and Orrin, too, need not speak, for me to know just how to finish this study for him. Up-stairs? You do not wish to go up-stairs? Ah, then, you miss the very cream of the house. I have worked with my own hand upon the rooms up-stairs, and there is a little Cupid wrought into the woodwork of a certain door which I greatly wish you to pass an opinion upon. I think the wings lack airiness, but the workmen swear it is as if he would fly from the door at a whisper. Come, Mistress Juliet; come, friend Orrin, if I lead the way you need not hesitate. Come! come!"

Was he alone? Were those eager steps of his unaccompanied, and should I not behold, if I looked within, the blooming face of Juliet and the frowning brows of Orrin, crowding close behind him as he moved? The fancy invoked by his words was so vivid, that for a moment I thought I should, and I never shall forget the thrill which seized me as I leaned forward and peered for one minute into the hall and saw there his solitary figure pausing on the lower step of the stairs, with that bend of the body which bespeaks an obeisance which is half homage and half an invitation. He was still talking, and as he went up, he looked back smiling and gossiping over his shoulder in a smooth and courtly way which made it impossible for me to withdraw my fascinated eyes.

"No banisters, sweet Juliet? Not yet—not yet; but Orrin will protect you from falling. No harm can come to you while he is at your side. Do you admire this sweep to the stairs? I saw a vision when I planned it, of a pretty woman coming down at the sound of her husband's step. The step has changed in sound to my imagination, but the pretty woman is prettier than ever, and will look her best as she comes down these stairs. Oh, that is a window-ledge for flowers. A honeymoon is nothing without flowers, and you must have forget-me-nots and pansies here till one cannot see from the window. You do not like such humble flowers? Fie! Mistress Juliet, it is hard to believe that,—even Orrin doubts it, as I see by his chiding air."

Here the gentle and bantering tones ceased, for he had reached the top of the stair. But in another moment I heard them again as he passed from room to room, pausing here and pausing there, till suddenly he gave a cheerful laugh, spoke her name in most inviting accents, and stepped into *that* room.

Then as if roused into galvanic action, I rose and followed, going up those midnight stairs and gaining the door where he had passed as if the impulse moving me had lent to my steps a certainty which preserved me from slipping even upon that dank and dangerous ascent. When in view of him again, I saw, as I had expected, that he was drawn up by the window and was bowing and beckoning with even more grace and suavity than he had shown below. "Will you not step out, Mistress Juliet?" he was saying; "I have a plan which I am anxious to submit to your judgment and which can only be decided upon from without. A high step true, but Orrin has lifted you over worse places and—and you will do me a great favor if only—" Here he gave a malignant shriek, and his countenance, from the most smiling and benignant expression, altered into that of a fiend from hell. "Ha, ha, ha!" he yelled. "She goes, and he is so fearful for her that he leaps after. That is a goodly stroke! Both—both—Crack! Ah, she looks at me, she looks—"

Silence and then a frozen figure crouching before my eyes, just the silence and just the figure I remembered seeing there twenty years before, only the face is older and the horror, if anything, greater. What did it mean? I tried to think, then as the full import of the scene burst upon me, and I realized that it was a murderer I was looking upon, and that Orrin, poor Orrin, had been innocent, I sank back and fell upon the floor, lost in the darkness of an utter unconsciousness.

I did not come to myself for hours; when I did I found myself alone in the old house.

* * * * *

Nothing was ever done to the Colonel, for when I came to tell my story the doctors said that the facts I related did not prove him to have been guilty of crime, as his condition was such that his own words could not be relied upon in a matter on which he had brooded more or less morbidly for years. So now when I see him pass through the churchyard or up and down the village street and note that he is affable as ever when he sees me, but growing more and more preoccupied with his own thoughts I do not know whether to look upon him with execration or profoundest pity, nor can any man guide me or satisfy my mind as to whether I should blame his jealousy or Orrin's pride for the pitiful tragedy which once darkened my life, and turned our pleasant village into a desert.

Of one thing only have I been made sure; that it was the Colonel who lit the brand which fired Orrin's cottage.

Anna Katharine Green

A MEMORABLE NIGHT

CHAPTER I

I am a young physician of limited practice and great ambition. At the time of the incidents I am about to relate, my office was in a respectable house in Twenty-fourth Street, New York City, and was shared, greatly to my own pleasure and convenience, by a clever young German whose acquaintance I had made in the hospital, and to whom I had become, in the one short year in which we had practised together, most unreasonably attached. I say unreasonably, because it was a liking for which I could not account even to myself, as he was neither especially prepossessing in appearance nor gifted with any too great amiability of character. He was, however, a brilliant theorist and an unquestionably trustworthy practitioner, and for these reasons probably I entertained for him a profound respect, and as I have already said a hearty and spontaneous affection.

As our specialties were the same, and as, moreover, they were of a nature which did not call for night-work, we usually spent the evening together. But once I failed to join him at the office, and it is of this night I have to tell.

I had been over to Orange, for my heart was sore over the quarrel I had had with Dora, and I was resolved to make one final effort towards reconciliation. But alas for my hopes, she was not at home; and, what was worse, I soon learned that she was going to sail the next morning for Europe. This news, coming as it did without warning, affected me seriously, for I knew if she escaped from my influence at this time, I should certainly lose her forever; for the gentleman concerning whom we had quarrelled, was a much better match for her than I, and almost equally in love. However, her father, who had always been my friend, did not look upon this same gentleman's advantages with as favorable an eye as she did, and when he heard I was in the house, he came hurrying into my presence, with excitement written in every line of his fine face.

"Ah, Dick, my boy," he exclaimed joyfully, "how opportune this is! I was wishing you would come, for, do you know, Appleby has taken passage on board the same steamer as Dora, and if he and she cross together, they will certainly come to an understanding, and that will not be fair to you, or pleasing to me; and I do not care who knows it!"

I gave him one look and sank, quite overwhelmed, into the seat nearest me. Appleby was the name of my rival, and I quite agreed with her father that the *tete-a-tetes* afforded by an ocean voyage would surely put an end to the hopes which I had so long and secretly cherished.

"Does she know he is going? Did she encourage him?" I stammered.

But the old man answered genially: "Oh, she knows, but I cannot say anything positive about her having encouraged him. The fact is, Dick, she still holds a soft place in her heart for you, and if you were going to be of the party—"

"Well?"

Anna Katharine Green

"I think you would come off conqueror yet."

"Then I will be of the party," I cried. "It is only six now, and I can be in New York by seven. That gives me five hours before midnight, time enough in which to arrange my plans, see Richter, and make everything ready for sailing in the morning."

"Dick, you are a trump!" exclaimed the gratified father. "You have a spirit I like, and if Dora does not like it too, then I am mistaken in her good sense. But can you leave your patients?"

"Just now I have but one patient who is in anything like a critical condition," I replied, "and her case Richter understands almost as well as I do myself. I will have to see her this evening of course and explain, but there is time for that if I go now. The steamer sails at nine?"

"Precisely."

"Do not tell Dora that I expect to be there; let her be surprised. Dear girl, she is quite well, I hope?"

"Yes, very well; only going over with her aunt to do some shopping. A poor outlook for a struggling physician, you think. Well, I don't know about that; she is just the kind of a girl to go from one extreme to another. If she once loves you she will not care any longer about Paris fashions."

"She shall love me," I cried, and left him in a great hurry, to catch the first train for Hoboken.

It seemed wild, this scheme, but I determined to pursue it. I loved Dora too much to lose her, and if three weeks' absence would procure me the happiness of my life, why should I hesitate to avail myself of the proffered opportunity. I rode on air as the express I had taken shot from station to station, and by the time I had arrived at Christopher Street Ferry my plans were all laid and my time disposed of till midnight.

It was therefore with no laggard step I hurried to my office, nor was it with any ordinary feelings of impatience that I found Richter out; for this was not his usual hour for absenting himself and I had much to tell him and many advices to give. It was the first balk I had received and I was fuming over it, when I saw what looked like a package of books lying on the table before me, and though it was addressed to my partner, I was about to take it up, when I heard my name uttered in a tremulous tone, and turning, saw a man standing in the doorway, who, the moment I met his eye, advanced into the room and said:

"O doctor, I have been waiting for you an hour. Mrs. Warner has been taken very bad, sir, and she prays that you will not delay a moment before coming to her. It is something serious I fear, and she may have died already, for she would have no one else but you, and it is now an hour since I left her."

"And who are you?" I asked, for though I knew Mrs. Warner well—she is the patient to whom I have already referred—I did not know her messenger.

"I am a servant in the house where she was taken ill."

"Then she is not at home?"

"No, sir, she is in Second Avenue."

"I am very sorry," I began, "but I have not the time—"

But he interrupted eagerly: "There is a carriage at the door;

we thought you might not have your phaeton ready."

I had noticed the carriage.

"Very well," said I. "I will go, but first let me write a line—"

"O sir," the man broke in pleadingly, "do not wait for anything. She is really very bad, and I heard her calling for you as I ran out of the house."

"She had her voice then?" I ventured, somewhat distrustful of the whole thing and yet not knowing how to refuse the man, especially as it was absolutely necessary for me to see Mrs. Warner that night and get her consent to my departure before I could think of making further plans.

So, leaving word for Richter to be sure and wait for me if he came home before I did, I signified to Mrs. Warner's messenger that I was ready to go with him, and immediately took a seat in the carriage which had been provided for me. The man at once jumped up on the box beside the driver, and before I could close the carriage door we were off, riding rapidly down Seventh Avenue.

As we went the thought came, "What if Mrs. Warner will not let me off!" But I dismissed the fear at once, for this patient of mine is an extremely unselfish woman, and if she were not too ill to grasp the situation, would certainly sympathize with the strait I was in and consent to accept Richter's services in place of my own, especially as she knows and trusts him.

When the carriage stopped it was already dark and I could distinguish little of the house I entered, save that it was large and old and did not look like an establishment where a man servant would be likely to be kept.

"Is Mrs. Warner here?" I asked of the man who was slowly getting down from the box.

"Yes, sir," he answered quickly; and I was about to ring the bell before me, when the door opened and a young German girl, courtesying slightly, welcomed me in, saying:

"Mrs. Warner is up-stairs, sir; in the front room, if you please."

Not doubting her, but greatly astonished at the barren aspect of the place I was in, I stumbled up the faintly lighted stairs before me and entered the great front room. It was empty, but through an open door at the other end I heard a voice saying: "He has come, madam"; and anxious to see my patient, whose presence in this desolate house I found it harder and harder to understand, I stepped into the room where she presumably lay.

Alas! for my temerity in doing so; for no sooner had I crossed the threshold than the door by which I had entered closed with a click unlike any I had ever heard before, and when I turned to see what it meant, another click came from the opposite side of the room, and I perceived, with a benumbed sense of wonder, that the one person whose somewhat shadowy figure I had encountered on entering had vanished from the place, and that I was shut up alone in a room without visible means of egress.

This was startling, and hard to believe at first, but after I had tried the door by which I had entered and found it securely locked, and then bounding to the other side of the room, tried the opposite one with the same result, I could not but acknowledge I was caught. What did it mean? Caught, and I was in haste, mad haste. Filling the room with my cries, I shouted for help and a quick release, but my efforts were naturally fruitless, and after exhausting myself in vain I stood still and surveyed, with what equanimity was left me, the appearance of the dreary place in which I had thus suddenly become entrapped.

CHAPTER II

It was a small square room, and I shall not soon forget with what a foreboding shudder I observed that its four blank walls were literally unbroken by a single window, for this told me that I was in no communication with the street, and that it would be impossible for me to summon help from the outside world. The single gas jet burning in a fixture hanging from the ceiling was the only relief given to the eye in the blank expanse of white wall that surrounded me; while as to furniture, the room could boast of nothing more than an old-fashioned black-walnut table and two chairs, the latter cushioned, but stiff in the back and generally dilapidated in appearance. The only sign of comfort about me was a tray that stood on the table, containing a couple of bottles of wine and two glasses. The bottles were full and the glasses clean, and to add to this appearance of hospitality a box of cigars rested invitingly near, which I could not fail to perceive, even at the first glance, were of the very best brand.

Astonished at these tokens of consideration for my welfare, and confounded by the prospect which they offered of a lengthy stay in this place, I gave another great shout; but to no better purpose than before. Not a voice answered, and not a stir was heard in the house. But there came from without the faint sound of suddenly moving wheels, as if the carriage which I had left standing before the door had slowly rolled away. If this were so, then was I indeed a prisoner, while the moments so necessary to my plans, and perhaps to the securing of my whole future happiness, were flying by like the wind. As I realized this, and my own utter helplessness, I fell into one of the chairs before me in a state of perfect despair. Not that any fears for my life were disturbing me, though one in my situation might well question if he would ever again breathe the open air from which he had been so ingeniously lured. I did not in that first moment of utter downheartedness so much as inquire the reason for the trick which had been played upon me. No, my heart was full of Dora, and I was asking myself if I were destined to lose her after all, and that through no lack of effort on my part, but just because a party of thieves or blackmailers had thought fit to play a game with my liberty.

It could not be; there must be some mistake about it; it was some great joke, or I was the victim of a dream, or suffering from some hideous nightmare. Why, only a half hour before I was in my own office, among my own familiar belongings, and now—But, alas, it was no delusion. Only four blank, whitewashed walls met my inquiring eyes, and though I knocked and knocked again upon the two doors which guarded me on either side, hollow echoes continued to be the only answer I received.

Had the carriage then taken away the two persons I had seen in this house, and was I indeed alone in its great emptiness? The thought made me desperate, but notwithstanding this I was resolved to continue my efforts, for I might be mistaken; there might yet be some being left who would yield to my entreaties if they were backed by something substantial.

Taking out my watch, I laid it on the table; it was just a quarter to eight. Then I emptied my trousers pockets of whatever money they held, and when all was heaped up before me, I could count but twelve dollars, which, together with my studs and a seal ring which I wore, seemed a paltry pittance with which to barter for the liberty of which I had been robbed. But it was all I had with me, and I was willing to part with it at once if only some one would unlock the door and let me go. But how to make known my wishes even if there was any one to listen to them? I had already called in vain, and there was no bell—yes, there was; why had I not seen it before? There was a bell and I sprang to ring it. But just as my hand fell on the cord, I heard a gentle voice behind my back saying in good English, but with a strong foreign accent:

"Put up your money, Mr. Atwater; we do not want your money, only your society. Allow me to beg you to replace both watch and money."

Wheeling about in my double surprise at the presence of this intruder and his unexpected acquaintance with my name, I encountered the smiling glance of a middle-aged man of genteel appearance and courteous manners. He was bowing almost to the ground, and was, as I instantly detected, of German birth and education, a gentleman, and not the blackleg I had every reason to expect to see.

"You have made a slight mistake," he was saying; "it is your society, only your society, that we want."

Astonished at his appearance, and exceedingly irritated by his words, I stepped back as he offered me my watch, and bluntly cried:

"If it is my society only that you want, you have certainly taken very strange means to procure it. A thief could have set no neater trap, and if it is money you want, state your sum and let me go, for my time is valuable and my society likely to be unpleasant."

He gave a shrug with his shoulders that in no wise interfered with his set smile.

"You choose to be facetious," he observed. "I have already remarked that we have no use for your money. Will you sit down? Here is some excellent wine, and if this brand of cigars does not suit you, I will send for another."

"Send for the devil!" I cried, greatly exasperated. "What do you mean by keeping me in this place against my will? Open that door and let me out, or—"

I was ready to spring and he saw it. Smiling more atrociously than ever, he slipped behind the table, and before I could reach him, had quietly drawn a pistol, which he cocked before my eyes.

"You are excited," he remarked, with a suavity that nearly drove me mad. "Now excitement is no aid to good company, and I am determined that none but good company shall be in this room to-night. So if you will be kind enough to calm yourself, Mr. Atwater, you and I may yet enjoy ourselves, but if not—" the action he made was significant, and I felt the cold sweat break out on my forehead through all the heat of my indignation.

But I did not mean to show him that he had intimidated me.

"Excuse me," said I, "and put down your pistol. Though you are making me lose irredeemable time, I will try and control myself enough to give you an opportunity for explaining yourself. Why have you entrapped me into this place?"

"I have already told you," said he, gently laying the pistol before him, but within easy reach of his hand.

"But that is preposterous," I began, fast losing my self-control again. "You do not know me, and if you did—"

"Pardon me, you see I know your name."

Yes, that was true, and the fact set me thinking. How did he know my name? I did not know him, nor did I know this house, or any reason for which I could have been beguiled into it. Was I the victim of a conspiracy, or was the man mad? Looking at him very earnestly, I declared:

"My name is Atwater, and so far you are right, but in learning that much about me you must also have learned that I am neither rich nor influential, nor of any special value to a blackmailer. Why choose me out then for—your society? Why not choose some one who can—talk?"

"I find your conversation very interesting."

Baffled, exasperated almost beyond the power to restrain myself, I shook my fist in his face, notwithstanding I saw his hand fly to his pistol.

"Let me go!" I shrieked. "Let me go out of this place. I have business, I tell you, important business which means everything to me, and which, if I do not attend to it to-night, will be lost to me for ever. Let me go, and I will so far reward you that I will speak to no one of what has taken place here to-night, but go my ways, forgetful of you, forgetful of this house, forgetful of all connected with it."

"You are very good," was his quiet reply, "but this wine has to be drunk." And he calmly poured out a glass, while I drew back in despair. "You do not drink wine?" he queried, holding up the glass he had filled between himself and the light. "It is a pity, for it is of most rare vintage. But perhaps you smoke?"

Sick and disgusted, I found a chair, and sat down in it. If the man were crazy, there was certainly method in his madness. Besides, he had not a crazy eye; there was calm calculation in it and not a little good-nature. Did he simply want to detain me, and if so, did he have a motive it would pay me to fathom before I exerted myself further to insure my release? Answering the wave he made me with his hand by reaching out for the bottle and filling myself a glass, I forced myself to speak more affably as I remarked:

"If the wine must be drunk, we had better be about it, as you cannot mean to detain me more than an hour, whatever reason you may have for wishing my society."

He looked at me inquiringly before answering, then tossing off his glass, he remarked:

"I am sorry, but in an hour a man can scarcely make the acquaintance of another man's exterior."

"Then you mean—"

"To know you thoroughly, if you will be so good; I may never have the opportunity again."

He must be mad; nothing else but mania could account for such words and such actions; and yet, if mad, why was he allowed to enter my presence? The man who brought me here, the woman who received me at the door, had not been mad.

"And I must stay here—" I began.

"Till I am quite satisfied. I am afraid that will take till morning."

I gave a cry of despair, and then in my utter desperation spoke up to him as I would to a man of feeling:

"You don't know what you are doing; you don't know what I shall suffer by any such cruel detention. This night is not like other nights to me. This is a special night in my life, and I need it, I need it, I tell you, to spend as I will. The woman I love"—it seemed horrible to speak of her in this place, but I was wild at my helplessness, and madly hoped I might awake some answering chord in a breast which could not be void of all feeling or he would not have that benevolent look in his eye—"the woman I love," I repeated, "sails for Europe to-morrow. We have quarrelled, but she still cares for me, and if I can sail on the same steamer, we will yet make up and be happy."

"At what time does this steamer start?"

"At nine in the morning."

"Well, you shall leave this house at eight. If you go directly to the steamer you will be in time."

"But—but," I panted, "I have made no arrangements. I shall have to go to my lodgings, write letters, get money. I ought to be there at this moment. Have you no mercy on a man who never did you wrong, and only asks to quit you and forget the precious hour you have made him lose?"

"I am sorry," he said, "it is certainly quite unfortunate, but the door will not be opened before eight. There is really no one in the house to unlock it."

"And do you mean to say," I cried aghast, "that you could not open that door if you would, that you are locked in here as well as I, and that I must remain here till morning, no matter how I feel or you feel?"

"Will you not take a cigar?" he asked.

Then I began to see how useless it was to struggle, and visions of Dora leaning on the steamer rail with that serpent whispering soft entreaties in her ear came rushing before me, till I could have wept in my jealous chagrin.

"It is cruel, base, devilish," I began. "If you had the excuse of wanting money, and took this method of wringing my all from me, I could have patience, but to entrap and keep me here for nothing, when my whole future happiness is trembling in the balance, is the work of a fiend and—" I made a sudden pause, for a strange idea had struck me.

CHAPTER III

What if this man, these men and this woman, were in league with him whose rivalry I feared, and whom I had intended to supplant on the morrow. It was a wild surmise, but was it any wilder than to believe I was held here for a mere whim, a freak, a joke, as this bowing, smiling man before me would have me believe?

Rising in fresh excitement, I struck my hand on the table. "You want to keep me from going on the steamer," I cried. "That other wretch who loves her has paid you—"

But that other wretch could not know that I was meditating any such unusual scheme, as following him without a full day's warning. I thought of this even before I had finished my sentence, and did not need the blank astonishment in the face of the man before me to convince me that I had given utterance to a foolish accusation. "It would have been some sort of a motive for your actions," I humbly added, as I sank back from my hostile attitude; "now you have none."

I thought he bestowed upon me a look of quiet pity, but if so he soon hid it with his uplifted glass.

"Forget the girl," said he; "I know of a dozen just as pretty."

I was too indignant to answer.

"Women are the bane of life," he now sententiously exclaimed. "They are ever intruding themselves between a man and his comfort, as for instance just now between yourself and this good wine."

I caught up the bottle in sheer desperation.

"Don't talk of them," I cried, "and I will try and drink. I almost wish there was poison in the glass. My death here might bring punishment upon you."

He shook his head, totally unmoved by my passion.

"We deal punishment, not receive it. It would not worry me in the least to leave you lying here upon the floor."

I did not believe this, but I did not stop to weigh the question then; I was too much struck by a word he had used.

"Deal punishment?" I repeated. "Are you punishing me? Is that why I am here?"

He laughed and held out his glass to mine.

"You enjoy being sarcastic," he observed. "Well, it gives a spice to conversation, I own. Talk is apt to be dull without it."

For reply I struck the glass from his hand; it fell and shivered, and he looked for the moment really distressed.

"I had rather you had struck me," he remarked, "for I have an answer for an injury like that; but for a broken glass—" He sighed and looked dolefully at the pieces on the floor.

Mortified and somewhat ashamed, I put down my own glass.

"You should not have exasperated me," I cried, and walked away beyond temptation, to the other side of the room.

His spirits had received a dampener, but in a few minutes he seized upon a cigar and began smoking; as the wreaths curled over his head he began to talk, and this time it was on subjects totally foreign to myself and even to himself. It was good talk; that I recognized, though I hardly listened to what he said. I was asking myself what time it had now got to be, and what was the meaning of my incarceration, till my brain became weary and I could scarcely distinguish the topic he discussed. But he kept on for all my seeming, and indeed real, indifference, kept on hour after hour in a monologue he endeavored to make interesting, and which probably would have been so if the time and occasion had been fit for my enjoying it. As it was, I had no ear for his choicest phrases, his subtlest criticisms, or his most philosophic disquisitions. I was wrapped up in self and my cruel disappointment, and when in a certain access of frenzy I leaped to my feet and took a look at the watch still lying on the table, and saw it was four o'clock in the morning, I gave a bound of final despair, and throwing myself on the floor, gave myself up to the heavy sleep that mercifully came to relieve me.

I was roused by feeling a touch on my breast. Clapping my hand to the spot where I had felt the intruding hand, I discovered that my watch had been returned to my pocket. Drawing it out I first looked at it and then cast my eyes quickly about the room. There was no one with me, and the doors stood open between me and the hall. It was eight o'clock, as my watch had just told me.

That I rushed from the house and took the shortest road to the steamer, goes without saying. I could not cross the ocean with Dora, but I might yet see her and tell her how near I came to giving her my company on that long voyage which now would only serve to further the ends of my rival. But when, after torturing delays on cars and ferry-boats, and incredible efforts to pierce a throng that was equally determined not to be pierced, I at last reached the wharf, it was to behold her, just as I had fancied in my wildest moments, leaning on a rail of the ship and listening, while she abstractedly waved her hand to some friends below, to the words of the man who had never looked so handsome to me or so odious as at this moment of his unconscious triumph. Her father was near her, and from his eager attitude and rapidly wandering gaze I saw that he was watching for me. At last he spied me struggling aboard, and immediately his face lighted up in a way which made me wish he had not thought it necessary to wait for my anticipated meeting with his daughter.

"Ah, Dick, you are late," he began, effusively, as I put foot on deck.

But I waved him back and went at once to Dora.

"Forgive me, pardon me," I incoherently said, as her sweet eyes rose in startled pleasure to mine. "I would have brought you flowers, but I meant to sail with you, Dora, I tried to— but wretches, villains, prevented it and—and—"

"Oh, it does not matter," she said, and then blushed, probably because the words sounded unkind, "I mean—"

But she could not say what she meant, for just then the bell rang for all visitors to leave, and her father came forward, evidently thinking all was right between us, smiled benignantly in her face, gave her a kiss and me a wink and disappeared in the crowd that was now rapidly going ashore.

I felt that I must follow, but I gave her one look and one squeeze of the hand, and then as I saw her glances wander to his face, I groaned in spirit, stammered some words of choking sorrow and was gone, before her embarrassment would let her speak words, which I knew would only add to my grief and make this hasty parting unendurable.

The look of amazement and chagrin with which her father met my reappearance on the dock can easily be imagined.

"Why, Dick," he exclaimed, "aren't you going after all? I thought I could rely on you. Where's your pluck, lad? Scared off by a frown? I wouldn't have believed it, Dick. What if she does frown to-day; she will smile to-morrow."

I shook my head; I could not tell him just then that it was not through any lack of pluck on my part that I had failed him.

When I left the dock I went straight to a restaurant, for I was faint as well as miserable. But my cup of coffee choked me and the rolls and eggs were more than I could face. Rising impatiently, I went out. Was any one more wretched than I that morning and could any one nourish a more bitter grievance? As I strode towards my lodgings I chewed the cud of my disappointment till my wrongs loomed up like mountains and I was seized by a spirit of revenge. Should I let such an interference as I had received go unpunished? No, if the wretch who had detained me was not used to punishment he should receive a specimen of it now and from a man who was no longer a prisoner, and who once aroused did not easily forego his purposes. Turning aside from my former destination, I went immediately to a police-station and when I had entered my complaint was astonished to see that all the officials had grouped about me and were listening to my words with the most startled interest.

"Was the man who came for you a German?" one asked.

I said "Yes."

"And the man who stood guardian over you and entertained you with wine and cigars, was not he a German too?"

I nodded acquiescence and they at once began to whisper together; then one of them advanced to me and said:

"You have not been home, I understand; you had better come."

Astonished by his manner I endeavored to inquire what he meant, but he drew me away, and not till we were within a stone's throw of my office did he say, "You must prepare yourself for a shock. The impertinences you suffered from last night were unpleasant no doubt, but if you had been allowed to return home, you might not now be deploring them in comparative peace and safety."

"What do you mean?"

"That your partner was not as fortunate as yourself. Look up at the house; what do you see there?"

A crowd was what I saw first, but he made me look higher, and then I perceived that the windows of my room, of our room, were shattered and blackened and that part of the casement of one had been blown out.

"A fire!" I shrieked. "Poor Richter was smoking—"

"No, he was not smoking. He had no time for a smoke. An infernal machine burst in that room last night and your friend was its wretched victim."

I never knew why my friend's life was made a sacrifice to the revenge of his fellow-countrymen. Though we had been intimate in the year we had been together, he had never talked to me of his country and I had never seen him in company with one of his own nation. But that he was the victim of some political revenge was apparent, for though it proved impossible to find the man who had detained me, the house was found and ransacked, and amongst other secret things was discovered the model of the machine which had been introduced into our room, and which had proved so fatal to the man it was addressed to. Why men who were so relentless in their purposes towards him should have taken such pains to keep me from sharing his fate, is one of those anomalies in human nature which now and then awake our astonishment. If I had not lost Dora through my detention at their hands I should look back upon that evening with sensations of thankfulness. As it is, I sometimes question if it would not have been better if they had let me take my chances.

*　*　*　*　*

Have I lost Dora? From a letter I received to-day I begin to think not.

THE BLACK CROSS

A black cross had been set against Judge Hawkins' name; why, it is not for me to say. We were not accustomed to explain our motives or to give reasons for our deeds. The deeds were enough, and this black cross meant death; and when it had been shown us, all that we needed to know further was at what hour we should meet for the contemplated raid.

A word from the captain settled that; and when the next Friday came, a dozen men met at the place of rendezvous, ready for the ride which should bring them to the Judge's solitary mansion across the mountains.

I was amongst them, and in as satisfactory a mood as I had ever been in my life; for the night was favorable, and the men hearty and in first-rate condition.

But after we had started, and were threading a certain wood, I began to have doubts. Feelings I had never before experienced assailed me with a force that first perplexed and then astounded me. I was afraid, and what rather heightened than diminished the unwonted sensation, was the fact that I was not afraid of anything tangible, either in the present or future, but of something unexplainable and peculiar, which, if it lay in the skies, certainly made them look dark indeed;

and if it hid in the forest, caused its faintest murmur to seem like the utterance of a great dread, as awful as it was inexplicable.

I nevertheless proceeded, and should have done so if the great streaks of lightning which now and then shot zigzag through the sky had taken the shape of words and bid us all beware. I was not one to be daunted, and knew no other course than that of advance when once a stroke of justice had been planned, and the direction for its fulfilment marked out. I went on, but I began to think, and that to me was an experience; for I had never been taught to reflect, only to fight and obey.

The house towards which we were riding was built on a hillside, and the first thing we saw on emerging from the forest, was a light burning in one of its distant windows. This was a surprise; for the hour was late, and in that part of the country people were accustomed to retire early, even such busy men as the Judge. He must have a visitor, and a visitor meant a possible complication of affairs; so a halt was called and I was singled out to reconnoitre the premises, and bring back word of what we had a right to expect.

I started off in a strange state of mind. The fear I had spoken of had left me, but a vague shadow remained, through which, as through a mist, I saw the light in that far away window beckoning me on to what I felt was in some way to make an end of my present life. As I drew nearer to it, the feeling increased; then it, too, left me, and I found myself once more the daring avenger. This was when I came to the foot of the hill and discovered I had but a few steps more to take.

The house, which had now become plainly visible, was a solid one of stone, built as I have said, on the hillside. It faced the road, as was shown by the large portico, dimly to

Anna Katharine Green

be discerned in that direction; but its rooms were mainly on the side, and it was from one of these that the light shone. As I came yet nearer, I perceived that these rooms were guarded by a piazza, which, communicating with the portico in front, afforded an open road to that window and a clear sight of what lay behind it.

I was instantly off my horse and upon the piazza, and before I had had time to realize that my fears had returned to me with double force, I had crept with stealthy steps towards that uncurtained window and looked in.

What did I see? At first nothing but a calm, studious figure, bending above a batch of closely written papers, upon which the light shone too brightly for me to perceive much of what lay beyond them. But gradually an influence, of whose workings I was scarcely conscious, drew my eyes away, and I began to discover on every side strange and beautiful objects which greatly interested me, until suddenly my eyes fell upon a vision of loveliness so enchanting that I forgot to look elsewhere, and became for the moment nothing but sight and feeling.

It was a picture, or so I thought in that first instant of awe and delight. But presently I saw that it was a woman, living and full of the thoughts that had never been mine; and at the discovery a sudden trembling seized me; for I had never seen anything in heaven or earth like her beauty, while she saw nothing but the man who was bending over his papers.

There was a door or something dark behind her, and against it her tall strong figure, clad in a close white gown, stood out with a distinctness that was not altogether earthly. But it was her face that held me, and made of me from moment to moment a new man.

For in it I discerned what I had never believed in till now, devotion that had no limit, and love which asked nothing in return. She seemed to be faltering on the threshold of that room, like one who would like to enter but does not dare, and in another moment, with a smile that pierced me through and through, she turned as if to go. Instantly I forgot everything but my despair, and leaned forward with an impetuosity that betrayed my presence, for she glanced quickly towards the window, and seeing me, turned pale, even while she rose in height till I felt myself shrink and grow small before her.

Thrusting out her hand, she caught from the table before her what looked like a small dagger, and holding it up, advanced upon me with blazing eyes and parted lips, not seeing that the Judge had risen to his feet, not seeing anything but my face glued against the pane, and staring with an expression that must have struck her to the heart as surely as her look pierced mine. When she was almost upon me I turned and fled. Hell could not have frightened me, but Heaven did; and for me that woman was Heaven whether she smiled or frowned, gazed upon another with love, or raised a dagger to strike me to the ground.

How soon I met my mates I cannot say. In a few minutes, doubtless, for they had stolen after me and had detected me running away from the window. I was forced to tell my tale, and I told it unhesitatingly, for I knew I could not save him—if I wanted to—and I knew I should save her or die in the attempt.

"He is alone there with a girl," I announced. "Whether she is his wife or not I cannot say, but there is no cross against her name, and I ask that she be spared not only from sharing his fate, but from the sight of his death, for she loves him."

This from me! No wonder the captain stared, then laughed. But I did not laugh in return, and being the strongest man in the band and the surest with my rifle, he did not trifle long, but listened to my plans and in part consented to them, so that I retreated to my post at the gateway with something like confidence, while he, approaching the door, lifted the knocker and let it fall with a resounding clang that must have rung like a knell of death to the hearts within.

For the Judge knew our errand. I saw it in his face when he rose to his feet, and he had no hope, for we had never failed in our attempts, and the house, though strongly built, was easily assailable.

*   *   *   *   *

While the captain knocked, three men had scaled the portico and were ready to enter the open windows, if the Judge refused to appear or offered any resistance to what was known as the captain's will.

"Death to the Judge!" was the cry; and it was echoed not only at the door, but around the house, where the rest of the men had drawn a cordon ready to waylay any one who sought to escape. Death to the Judge! And the Judge was loved by that woman and would be mourned by her till—But a voice is speaking, a voice from out that great house, and it asks what is wanted and what the meaning is of these threats of death.

And the captain answers short and sharp:

"The Ku-Klux commands but never explains. What it commands now is for Judge Hawkins to come forth. If he shrinks or delays his house will be entered and burnt; but if he will come out and meet like a man what awaits him, his house shall go free and his family remain unmolested."

"And what is it that awaits him?" pursued the voice.

"Four bullets from four unerring rifles," returned the captain.

"It is well; he will come forth," cried the voice, and then in a huskier tone: "Let me kiss the woman I love. I will not keep you long."

And the captain answered nothing, only counted out clearly and steadily, "One—two—three," up to a hundred, then he paused, turned, and lifted his hand; when instantly our four rifles rose, and at the same moment the door, with a faint grating sound I shall never forget, slowly opened and the firm, unshrinking figure of the Judge appeared.

We did not delay. One simultaneous burst of fire, one loud quick crack, and his figure fell before our eyes. A sound, a cry from within, then all was still, and the captain, mounting his horse, gave one quick whistle and galloped away. We followed him, but I was the last to mount, and did not follow long; for at the flash of those guns I had seen a smile cross our victim's lip, and my heart was on fire, and I could not rest till I had found my way back to that open doorway and the figure lying within it.

There it was, and behind it a house empty as my heart has been since that day. A man's dress covering a woman's form—and over the motionless, perfect features, that same smile which I had seen in the room beyond and again in the quick glare of the rifles.

I had harbored no evil thought concerning her, but when I beheld that smile now sealed and fixed upon her lips, I found the soul I had never known I possessed until that day.

Anna Katharine Green

A MYSTERIOUS CASE

It was a mystery to me, but not to the other doctors. They took, as was natural, the worst possible view of the matter, and accepted the only solution which the facts seem to warrant. But they are men, and I am a woman; besides, I knew the nurse well, and I could not believe her capable of wilful deceit, much less of the heinous crime which deceit in this case involved. So to me the affair was a mystery.

The facts were these:

My patient, a young typewriter, seemingly without friends or enemies, lay in a small room of a boarding-house, afflicted with a painful but not dangerous malady. Though she was comparatively helpless, her vital organs were strong, and we never had a moment's uneasiness concerning her, till one morning when we found her in an almost dying condition from having taken, as we quickly discovered, a dose of poison, instead of the soothing mixture which had been left for her with the nurse. Poison! and no one, not even herself or the nurse, could explain how the same got into the room, much less into her medicine. And when I came to study the situation, I found myself as much at loss as they; indeed, more so; for I knew I had made no mistake in preparing the mixture, and that, even if I had, this especial poison could not have found its way into it, owing to the fact that there neither was nor ever had been a drop of it in my possession.

The mixture, then, was pure when it left my hand, and, according to the nurse, whom, as I have said, I implicitly believe, it went into the glass pure. And yet when, two hours later, without her having left the room or anybody coming into it, she found occasion to administer the draught, poison was in the cup, and the patient was only saved from death by the most immediate and energetic measures, not only on her part, but on that of Dr. Holmes, whom in her haste and perturbation she had called in from the adjacent house.

The patient, young, innocent, unfortunate, but of a strangely courageous disposition, betrayed nothing but the utmost surprise at the peril she had so narrowly escaped. When Dr. Holmes intimated that perhaps she had been tired of suffering, and had herself found means of putting the deadly drug into her medicine, she opened her great gray eyes, with such a look of child-like surprise and reproach, that he blushed, and murmured some sort of apology.

"Poison myself?" she cried, "when you promise me that I shall get well? You do not know what a horror I have of dying in debt, or you would never say that."

This was some time after the critical moment had passed, and there were in the room Mrs. Dayton, the landlady, Dr. Holmes, the nurse, and myself. At the utterance of these words we all felt ashamed and cast looks of increased interest at the poor girl.

She was very lovely. Though without means, and to all appearance without friends, she possessed in great degree the charm of winsomeness, and not even her many sufferings, nor the indignation under which she was then laboring, could quite rob her countenance of that tender and confiding expression which so often redeems the plainest face and makes beauty doubly attractive.

"Dr. Holmes does not know you," I hastened to say; "I do, and utterly repel for you any such insinuation. In return, will you tell me if there is any one in the world whom you can call your enemy? Though the chief mystery is how so deadly and unusual a poison could have gotten into a clean glass, without the knowledge of yourself or the nurse, still it might not be amiss to know if there is any one, here or elsewhere, who for any reason might desire your death."

The surprise in the child-like eyes increased rather than diminished.

"I don't know what to say," she murmured. "I am so insignificant and feeble a person that it seems absurd for me to talk of having an enemy. Besides, I have none. On the contrary, every one seems to love me more than I deserve. Haven't you noticed it, Mrs. Dayton?"

The landlady smiled and stroked the sick girl's hand.

"Indeed," she replied, "I have noticed that people love you, but I have never thought that it was more than you deserved. You are a dear little thing, Addie."

And though she knew and I knew that the "every one" mentioned by the poor girl meant ourselves, and possibly her unknown employer, we were none the less touched by her words. The more we studied the mystery, the deeper and less explainable did it become.

And indeed I doubt if we should have ever got to the bottom of it, if there had not presently occurred in my patient a repetition of the same dangerous symptoms, followed by the same discovery, of poison in the glass, and the same failure on the part of herself and nurse to account for it. I was aroused from my bed at midnight to attend her, and as I entered her room and met her beseeching eyes looking upon me from the very shadow of death, I made a vow that I would never cease my efforts till I had penetrated the secret of what certainly looked like a persistent attempt upon this poor girl's life.

I went about the matter deliberately. As soon as I could leave her side, I drew the nurse into a corner and again questioned her. The answers were the same as before. Addie had shown distress as soon as she had swallowed her usual quantity of medicine, and in a few minutes more was in a perilous condition.

"Did you hand the glass yourself to Addie?"

"I did."

"Where did you take it from?"

"From the place where you left it—the little stand on the farther side of the bed."

"And do you mean to say that you had not touched it since I prepared it?"

"I do, ma'am."

"And that no one else has been in the room?"

"No one, ma'am."

I looked at her intently. I trusted her, but the best of us are but mortal.

"Can you assure me that you have not been asleep during this time?"

"Look at this letter I have been writing," she returned. "It is eight pages long, and it was not begun when you left us at 10 o'clock."

I shook my head and fell into a deep revery. How was that matter to be elucidated, and how was my patient to be saved? Another draught of this deadly poison, and no power on earth could resuscitate her. What should I do, and with what weapons should I combat a danger at once so subtle and so deadly? Reflection brought no decision, and I left the room at last, determined upon but one point, and that was the immediate removal of my patient. But before I had left the house I changed my mind even on this point. Removal of the patient meant safety to her, perhaps, but not the explanation of her mysterious poisoning. I would change the position of her bed, and I would even set a watch over her and the nurse, but I would not take her out of the house—not yet.

And what had produced this change in my plans? The look of a woman whom I met on the stairs. I did not know her, but when I encountered her glance I felt that there was some connection between us, and I was not at all surprised to hear her ask:

"And how is Miss Wilcox to-day?"

"Miss Wilcox is very low," I returned. "The least neglect, the least shock to her nerves, would be sufficient to make all my efforts useless. Otherwise—"

"She will get well?"

I nodded. I had exaggerated the condition of the sufferer, but some secret instinct compelled me to do so. The look which passed over the woman's face satisfied me that I had done well; and, though I left the house, it was with the intention of speedily returning and making inquiries into the woman's character and position in the household.

I learned little or nothing. That she occupied a good room and paid for it regularly seemed to be sufficient to satisfy Mrs. Dayton. Her name, which proved to be Leroux, showed her to be French, and her promptly paid $10 a week showed her to be respectable—what more could any hard-working landlady require? But I was distrustful. Her face, though handsome, possessed an eager, ferocious look which I could not forget, and the slight gesture with which she had passed me at the close of the short conversation I have given above had a suggestion of triumph in it which seemed to contain whole volumes of secret and mysterious hate. I went into Miss Wilcox's room very thoughtful.

"I am going—"

But here the nurse held up her hand. "Hark," she whispered; she had just set the clock, and was listening to its striking.

I did hark, but not to the clock.

"Whose step is that?" I asked, after she had left the clock, and sat down.

"Oh, some one in the next room. The walls here are very thin—only boards in places."

I did not complete what I had begun to say. If I could hear steps through the partition, then could our neighbors hear us talk, and what I had determined upon must be kept secret from all outsiders. I drew a sheet of paper toward me and wrote:

Anna Katharine Green

"I shall stay here to-night. Something tells me that in doing this I shall solve this mystery. But I must appear to go. Take my instructions as usual, and bid me good-night. Lock the door after me, but with a turn of the key instantly unlock it again. I shall go down stairs, see that my carriage drives away, and quietly return. On my re-entrance I shall expect to find Miss Wilcox on the couch with the screen drawn up around it, you in your big chair, and the light lowered. What I do thereafter need not concern you. Pretend to go to sleep."

The nurse nodded, and immediately entered upon the programme I had planned. I prepared the medicine as usual, placed it in its usual glass, and laid that glass where it had always been set, on a small table at the farther side of the bed. Then I said "Good-night," and passed hurriedly out.

I was fortunate enough to meet no one, going or coming. I regained the room, pushed open the door, and finding everything in order, proceeded at once to the bed, upon which, after taking off my hat and cloak and carefully concealing them, I lay down and deftly covered myself up.

My idea was this—that by some mesmeric influence of which she was ignorant, the nurse had been forced to either poison the glass herself or open the door for another to do it. If this were so, she or the other person would be obliged to pass around the foot of the bed in order to reach the glass, and I should be sure to see it, for I did not pretend to sleep. By the low light enough could be discerned for safe movement about the room, and not enough to make apparent the change which had been made in the occupant of the bed. I waited with indescribable anxiety, and more than once fancied I heard steps, if not a feverish breathing close to my bed-head; but no one appeared, and the nurse in her big chair did not move.

At last I grew weary, and fearful of losing control over my eyelids, I fixed my gaze upon the glass, as if in so doing I should find a talisman to keep me awake, when, great God! what was it I saw! A hand, a creeping hand coming from nowhere and joined to nothing, closing about that glass and drawing it slowly away till it disappeared entirely from before my eyes!

I gasped—I could not help it—but I did not stir. For now I knew I was asleep and dreaming. But no, I pinch myself under the clothes, and find that I am very wide awake indeed; and then—look! look! the glass is returning; the hand—a woman's hand—is slowly setting it back in its place, and—

With a bound I have that hand in my grasp. It is a living hand, and it is very warm and strong and fierce, and the glass has fallen and lies shattered between us, and a double cry is heard, one from behind the partition, through an opening in which this hand had been thrust, and one from the nurse, who has jumped to her feet and is even now assisting me in holding the struggling member, upon which I have managed to scratch a tell-tale mark with a piece of the fallen glass. At sight of the iron-like grip which this latter lays upon the intruding member, I at once release my own grasp.

"Hold on," I cried, and leaping from the bed, I hastened first to my patient, whom I carefully reassured, and then into the hall, where I found the landlady running to see what was the matter. "I have found the wretch," I cried, and drawing her after me, hurried about to the other side of the partition, where I found a closet, and in it the woman I had met on the stairs, but glaring now like a tiger in her rage, menace, and fear.

That woman was my humble little patient's bitter but

unknown enemy. Enamoured of a man who—unwisely, perhaps—had expressed in her hearing his admiration for the pretty typewriter, she had conceived the idea that he intended to marry the latter, and, vowing vengeance, had taken up her abode in the same house with the innocent girl, where, had it not been for the fortunate circumstance of my meeting her on the stairs, she would certainly have carried out her scheme of vile and secret murder. The poison she had bought in another city, and the hole in the partition she had herself cut. This had been done at first for the purpose of observation, she having detected in passing by Miss Wilcox's open door that a banner of painted silk hung over that portion of the wall in such a way as to hide any aperture which might be made there.

Afterward, when Miss Wilcox fell sick, and she discovered by short glimpses through her loop-hole that the glass of medicine was placed on a table just under this banner, she could not resist the temptation to enlarge the hole to a size sufficient to admit the pushing aside of the banner and the reaching through of her murderous hand. Why she did not put poison enough in the glass to kill Miss Wilcox at once I have never discovered. Probably she feared detection. That by doing as she did she brought about the very event she had endeavored to avert, is the most pleasing part of the tale. When the gentleman of whom I have spoken learned of the wicked attempt which had been made upon Miss Wilcox's life, his heart took pity upon her, and a marriage ensued, which I have every reason to believe is a happy one.

SHALL HE WED HER?

When I met Taylor at the Club the other night, he looked so cheerful I scarcely knew him.

"What is it?" cried I, advancing with outstretched hand.

"I am going to be married," was his gay reply. "This is my last night at the Club."

I was glad, and showed it. Taylor is a man for whom domestic life is a necessity. He has never been at home with us, though we all liked him, and he in his way liked us.

"And who is the fortunate lady?" I inquired; for I had been out of town for some time, and had not as yet been made acquainted with the latest society news.

"My intended bride is Mrs. Walworth, the young widow—"

He must have seen a change take place in my expression, for he stopped.

"You know her, of course?" he added, after a careful study of my face.

I had by this time regained my self-possession.

"Of course," I repeated, "and I have always thought her one of the most attractive women in the city. Another shake upon it, old man."

But my heart was heavy and my mind perplexed notwithstanding the forced cordiality of my tones, and I took an early opportunity to withdraw by myself and think over the situation.

Mrs. Walworth? She is a pretty woman, and what is more, she is to all appearance a woman whose winning manners bespeak a kindly heart. "Just the person," I contemplated, "whom I would pick out for the helpmate of my somewhat exacting friend, if—" I paused on that if. It was a formidable one and grew none the smaller or less important under my broodings. Indeed, it seemed to dilate until it assumed gigantic proportions, worrying me and weighing so heavily upon my conscience that I at last rose from the newspaper at which I had been hopelessly staring, and looking up Taylor again asked him how soon he expected to become a benedict.

His answer startled me. "In a week," he replied, "and if I have not asked you to the ceremony it is because Helen is not in a position to—"

I suppose he finished the sentence, but I did not hear him. If the marriage was so near, of course it would be folly on my part to attempt to hinder it. I drew off for the second time.

But I could not remain easy. Taylor is a good fellow, and it would be a shame to allow him to marry a woman with whom he could never be happy. He would feel any such disappointment so keenly, so much more keenly than most men. A lack of principle or even of sensibility on her part would make him miserable. Anticipating heaven, he would not need a hell to make him wretched; a purgatory would do it. Was I right then in letting him proceed in his intentions regarding Mrs. Walworth, when she possibly was the woman who—I paused and tried to call up her countenance before me. It was a sweet one and possibly a true one. I might have trusted her for myself, but I do not look for perfection, and Taylor does, and will certainly go to the bad if he is deceived in his expectations. But in a week! It is too late for interference—only it is never too late till the knot is tied. As I thought of this, I decided impulsively, and perhaps you may say unwisely, to give him a hint of his danger, and I did it in this wise:

"Taylor," said I, when I had him safely in my own rooms, "I am going to tell you a bit of personal history, curious enough, I think, to interest you even upon the eve of your marriage. I do not know when I shall see you again, and I should like you to know how a lawyer and man of the world can sometimes be taken in."

He nodded, accepting the situation good-humoredly, though I saw by the abstraction with which he gazed into the fire that I should have to be very interesting to lure him from the thoughts that engrossed him. As I meant to be very interesting, this did not greatly concern me.

"One morning last spring," I began, "I received in my morning mail a letter, the delicate penmanship of which at once attracted my attention and awakened my curiosity. Turning to the signature, I read the name of a young lady friend of mine, and somewhat startled at the thought that this was the first time I had ever seen the handwriting of one I knew so well, I perused the letter with an interest that presently became painful as I realized the tenor of its contents. I will not quote the letter, though I could, but confine myself to saying that after a modest recognition of my friendship for her—quite a fatherly friendship, I assure you, as she is only eighteen, and I, as you know, am well on towards fifty—she proceeded to ask in a humble and confiding spirit for the loan—do not start—of fifty dollars. Such a request coming from a young girl well connected and with every visible sign of being generously provided for by her father, was certainly startling to an old bachelor of settled ways and strict notions, but remembering her youth and the childish innocence of her manner, I turned over the page and read as her reason for proffering such a request, that her heart was set upon aiding a certain poor family that stood in immediate need of food, clothes, and medicines, but that she could not do what she wished, because she had already spent all the money allowed her by her father for such purposes and dared not go to him for more, as she had once before offended him by doing this, and feared if she repeated her fault he would carry out the threat he had then made of stopping her allowance altogether. But the family was a deserving one and she could not see any member of it starve, so she came to me, of whose goodness she was assured, convinced I would understand her perplexity and excuse her, and so forth and so forth, in language quite child-like and entreating, which, if it did not satisfy my ideas of propriety, at least touched my heart and made any action which I could take in the matter extremely difficult.

"To refuse her request would be at once to mortify and aggrieve her; to accede to it and give her the fifty dollars she asked—a sum by the way I could not well spare—would be to encourage an action easily pardoned once, but which if repeated would lead to unpleasant complications, to say the least. The third course, of informing her father of what she needed, I did not even consider, for I knew him well enough to be sure that nothing but pain to her would be the result. I therefore compromised the affair by inclosing the money in a letter, in which I told her that I comprehended her difficulty and sent with pleasure the amount she needed, but that as a friend I must add that while in the present instance she had run no risk of being misunderstood or unkindly censured, that such a request made to another man and under other circumstances might provoke a surprise capable of leading to the most unpleasant consequences, and advised her if she ever again found herself in such a strait to appeal directly to her father, or else to deny herself a charity which she was in no position to bestow.

"This letter I undertook to deliver myself, for one of the curious points of her communication had been the entreaty that I would not delay the help she needed by trusting the money to any hand but my own, but would bring it to a certain hotel down-town and place it at the beginning of the book of Isaiah in the large Bible I would find lying on a side table in the small parlor off the main one. She would seek it there before the morning was over, and so, without the intervention of a third party, acquire the means she desired for helping a poor and deserving family.

"I knew the hotel she mentioned, and I remembered the room, but I did not remember the Bible. However, it was sure to be in the place she indicated; and though I was not in much sympathy with my errand, I respected her whim and carried the letter down-town. I had reached Main Street and was in sight of the hotel designated, when suddenly on the opposite corner of the street I saw the young girl herself. She looked as fresh as the morning, and smiled so gayly I felt somewhat repaid for the annoyance she had caused me, and gratified that I could cut matters short by putting the letter directly in her hand, I crossed the street to her side. As soon as we were face to face, I said:

"'How fortunate I am to meet you. Here is the amount you need sealed up in this letter. You see I had it all ready.'"

"The face she lifted to mine wore so blank a look that I paused, astonished."

"'What do you mean?' she asked, her eyes looking straight into mine with such innocence in their clear blue depths, I was at once convinced she knew nothing of the matter with which my thoughts were busy. 'I am very glad to see you, but I do not in the least understand what you mean by the amount I need.' And she glanced at the letter I held out, with an air of distrust mingled with curiosity.

"'You cut me short in my efforts to do a charitable action. I heard, no matter how, that you were interested just now in a destitute family, and took this way of assisting you in their behalf.'"

"Her blue eyes opened wider. 'The poor are always with us,' she replied, 'but I know of no especial family just now that requires any such help as you intimate. If I did, papa would give me what assistance I needed.'"

"I was greatly pleased to hear her say this, for I am very fond of my young friend, but I was deeply indignant also against the unknown person who had taken advantage of my regard for this young girl to force money from me. I therefore did not linger at her side, but after due apologies hastened immediately here where there is a man employed who to my knowledge had once been a trusted member of the police.

"Telling him no more of the story than was necessary to ensure his co-operation in the plan I had formed to discover the author of this fraud, I extracted the bank-notes from the letter I had written, and put in their place stiff pieces of manila paper. Taking the envelope so filled to the hotel already referred to, I placed it at the opening chapters of Isaiah in the Bible, as described. There was no one in any of the rooms when I went in, and I encountered only a bell-boy as I came out, but at the door I ran against a young man whom I strictly forbore to recognize, but whom I knew to be my improvised detective coming to take his stand in some place where he could watch the parlor and note who went into it.

"At noon I returned to the hotel, passed immediately to the small parlor and looked into the Bible. The letter was gone. Coming out of the room, I was at once joined by my detective.

"'Has the letter been taken?' he eagerly inquired."

"I nodded."

"His brows wrinkled and he looked both troubled and perplexed."

"'I don't understand it,' he remarked. 'I've seen every one who has gone into that room since you left it, but I do not know any more than before who took the letter. You see,' he continued, as I looked at him sharply, 'I had to remain out here. If I had gone even into the large room, the Bible would not have been disturbed, nor the letter either. So, in the hope of knowing the rogue at sight, I strolled about this hall, and kept my eye constantly on that door, but—'"

"He looked embarrassed, and stopped. 'You say the letter is gone,' he suggested, after a moment."

"'Yes,' I returned."

"He shook his head. 'Nobody went into that room or came out of it,' he went on, 'whom you would have wished me to follow. I should have thought myself losing time if I had taken one step after any one of them.'"

"'But who did go into that room?' I urged, impatient at his perplexity."

"'Only three persons this morning,' he returned. 'You know them all.' And he mentioned first Mrs. Couldock."

Taylor, who was lending me the superficial attention of a preoccupied man, smiled frankly at the utterance of this name. "Of course, she had nothing to do with such a debasing piece of business," he observed.

"Of course not," I repeated. "Nor does it seem likely that Miss Dawes could have been concerned in it. Yet my detective told me that she was the next person who went into the parlor."

"I do not know Miss Dawes so well," remarked Taylor, carelessly.

"But I do," said I; "and I would as soon suspect my sister of a dishonorable act as this noble, self-sacrificing woman."

"The third person?" suggested Taylor.

I got up and crossed the floor. When my back was to him, I said, quietly—"was Mrs. Walworth."

The silence that followed was very painful. I did not care to break it, and he, doubtless, found himself unable to do so. It must have been five minutes before either of us spoke; then he suddenly cried:

"Where is that detective, as you call him? I want to see him."

"Let me see him for you," said I. "I should hardly wish Sudley, discreet as I consider him, to know you had any interest in this affair."

Taylor rose and came to where I stood.

"You believe," said he, "that she, the woman I am about to marry, is the one who wrote you that infamous letter?"

I faced him quite frankly. "I do not feel ready to acknowledge that," I replied. "One of those three women took my letter out from the Bible, where I placed it; which of them wrote the lines that provoked it I do not dare conjecture. You say it was not Mrs. Couldock, I say it was not Miss Dawes, but—"

He broke in upon me impetuously.

"Have you the letter?" he asked.

I had, and showed it to him.

"It is not Helen's handwriting," he said.

"Nor is it that of Mrs. Couldock or Miss Dawes."

He looked at me for a moment in a wild sort of way.

"You think she got some one to write it for her?" he cried. "Helen! my Helen! But it is not so; it cannot be so. Why, Huntley, to have sent such a letter as that over the name of an innocent young girl, who, but for the happy chance of meeting you as she did might never have had the opportunity of righting herself in your estimation, argues a cold and calculating selfishness closely allied to depravity. And my Helen is an angel—or so I have always thought her."

The depth to which his voice sank in the last sentence showed that for all his seeming confidence he was not without his doubts.

I began to feel very uncomfortable, and not knowing what consolation to offer, I ventured upon the suggestion that he should see Mrs. Walworth and frankly ask her whether she had been to the hotel on Main Street on such a day, and if so, if she had seen a letter addressed to Miss N—lying on the table of the small parlor. His answer showed how much his confidence in her had been shaken.

"A woman who, for the sake of paying some unworthy debt or of gratifying some whim of feminine vanity, could make use of a young girl's signature to obtain money, would not hesitate at any denial. She would not even blench at my questions."

He was right.

"I must be convinced in some other way," he went on. "Mrs. Couldock or Miss Dawes do not either of them possess any more truthful or ingenuous countenance than she does, and though it seems madness to suspect such women—"

"Wait," I broke in. "Let us be sure of all the facts before we go on. You lie down here and close your eyes; now pull the rug up so. I will have Sudley in and question him. If you do not turn towards the light he will not know who you are."

Taylor followed my suggestion, and in a few moments Sudley stood before me. I opened upon him quite carelessly.

"Sudley," said I, throwing down the newspaper I had been ostensibly reading, "you remember that little business you did for me in Main Street last month? Something I've been reading made me think of it again."

"Yes, sir."

"Have you never had a conviction yourself as to which of the three ladies you saw go into the parlor took the letter I left hid in the Bible?"

"No, sir. You see I could not. All of them are well known in society here and all of them belong to the most respectable families. I wouldn't dare to choose between them, sir."

"Certainly not," I rejoined, "unless you have some good reason for doing so, such as having been able to account for the visits of two of the ladies to the hotel, and not of the third."

"They all had a good pretext for being there. Mrs. Couldock gave her card to the boy before going into the parlor, and left as soon as he returned with word that the lady she called to see was not in. Miss Dawes gave no card, but asked for a Miss Terhune, I think, and did not remain a moment after she was informed that that lady had left the hotel."

"And Mrs. Walworth?"

"She came in from the street adjusting her veil, and upon looking around for a mirror was directed to the parlor, into which she at once stepped. She remained there but a moment, and when she came out passed directly into the street."

These words disconcerted me; the mirror was just over the table in the small room, but I managed to remark nonchalantly:

Anna Katharine Green

"Could you not tell whether any of these three ladies opened the Bible?"

"Not without seeming intrusive."

I sighed and dismissed the man. When he was gone I approached Taylor.

"He can give us no assistance," I cried.

My friend was already on his feet, looking very miserable.

"I know of only one thing to do," he remarked. "To-morrow I shall call upon Mrs. Couldock and Miss Dawes, and entreat them to tell me if, for any reason, they undertook to deliver a letter mysteriously left in the Bible of the—Hotel one day last month. They may have been deputed to do so, and be quite willing to acknowledge it."

"And Mrs. Walworth? Will you not ask her the same question?"

He shook his head and turned away.

"Very well," said I to myself, "then I will."

Accordingly the next day I called upon Mrs. Walworth.

Taking her by the hand, I gently forced her to stand for a moment where the light from the one window fell full upon her face. I said:

"You must pardon my intrusion upon you at a time when you are naturally so busy, but there is something you can do for me that will rid me of a great anxiety. You remember being in—Hotel one morning last month?"

She was looking quietly up at me, her lips parted, her eyes smiling and expectant, but at the mention of that hotel I thought—and yet I may have been mistaken—that a slight change took place in her expression, if it was only that the glance grew more gentle and the smile more marked.

But her voice when she answered was the same as that with which she had uttered her greeting.

"I do not remember," she replied, "yet I may have been there; I go to so many places. Why do you ask?" she inquired.

"Because if you were there on that morning—and I have been told you were—you may be able to solve a question that is greatly perplexing me."

Still the same gentle, inquiring look on her face; only now there was a little furrow of wonder or interest between the eyes.

"I had business in that hotel on that morning," I continued. "I had left a letter for a young friend of mine in the Bible that lies on the small table of the inner parlor, and as she never received it I have been driven into making all kinds of inquiries in the hope of finding some explanation of the fact. As you were there at the time you may have seen something that would aid me. Is it not possible, Mrs. Walworth?"

Her smile, which had faded, reappeared. On the lips which Taylor so much admired a little pout became visible, and she looked quite enchanting.

"I do not even remember being at that hotel at all," she protested. "Did Mr. Taylor say I was there?" she inquired, with just that added look of exquisite naeivete which the utterance of a lover's name should call up on the face of a prospective bride.

"No," I answered gravely; "Mr. Taylor, unhappily, was not with you that morning." She looked startled.

"Unhappily," she repeated. "What do you mean by that word?" And she drew back looking very much displeased.

I had expected this, and so was not thrown off my guard.

"I mean," I proceeded calmly, "that if you had had such a companion with you on that morning I should now be able to put my questions to him, instead of taking your time and interrupting your affairs by my importunities."

"You will tell me just what you mean," said she, earnestly.

I was equally emphatic in my reply. "That is only just. You ought to know why I trouble you with this matter. It is because this letter of which I speak was taken from its hiding-place by some one who went into the hotel parlor between the hours of 10:30 and 12 o'clock, and as to my certain knowledge only three persons crossed its threshold on that especial morning at that especial time, I naturally appeal to each of them in turn for an answer to the problem that is troubling me. You know Miss N—. Seeing by accident a letter addressed to her lying in a Bible in a strange hotel, you might have thought it your duty to take it out and carry it to her. If you did and if you lost it—"

"But I didn't," she interrupted, warmly. "I know nothing about any such letter, and if you had not declared so positively that I was in that hotel on that especial day I should be tempted to deny that too, for I have no recollection of going there last month."

"Not for the purpose of rearranging a veil that had been blown off?"

"Oh!" she said, but as one who recalls a forgotten fact, not as one who is tripped up in an evasion.

I began to think her innocent, and lost some of the gloom which had been oppressing me.

"You remember now?" said I.

"Oh, yes, I remember that."

Her manner so completely declared that her acknowledgments stopped there, I saw it would be useless to venture further. If she were innocent she could not tell more, if she were guilty she would not; so, feeling that the inclination of my belief was in favor of the former hypothesis, I again took her hand, and said:

"I see that you can give me no help. I am sorry, for the whole happiness of a man, and perhaps that of a woman also, depends upon the discovery as to who took the letter from out the Bible where I had hidden it on that unfortunate morning." And, making her another low bow, I was about to take my departure, when she grasped me impulsively by the arm.

"What man?" she whispered; and in a lower tone still, "What woman?"

I turned and looked at her. "Great heaven!" thought I, "can such a face hide a selfish and intriguing heart?" and in a flash I summoned up in comparison before me the plain, honest, and reliable countenance of Mrs. Couldock and that of the comely and unpretending Miss Dawes, and knew not what to think.

"You do not mean yourself?" she continued, as she met my look of distress.

"No," I returned; "happily for me my welfare is not bound up in the honor of any woman." And leaving that shaft to work its way into her heart, if that heart were vulnerable, I took my leave, more troubled and less decided than when I entered.

For her manner had been absolutely that of a woman surprised by insinuations she was too innocent to rate at their real importance. And yet, if she did not take away that letter, who did? Mrs. Couldock? Impossible. Miss Dawes? The thought was untenable, even for an instant. I waited in great depression of spirits for the call I knew Taylor would not fail to make that evening.

When he came I saw what the result of my revelations was likely to be as plainly as I see it now. He had conversed frankly with Mrs. Couldock and with Miss Dawes, and was perfectly convinced as to the utter ignorance of them both in regard to the whole affair. In consequence, Mrs. Walworth was guilty in his estimation, and being held guilty could be no wife for him, much as he had loved her, and urgent as may have been the cause for her act.

"But," said I, in some horror of the consequences of an interference for which I was almost ready to blame myself now, "Mrs. Couldock and Miss Dawes could have done no more than deny all knowledge of this letter. Now Mrs. Walworth does that, and—"

"You have seen her? You have asked her—"

"Yes, I have seen her, and I have asked her, and not an eyelash drooped as she affirmed a complete ignorance of the whole affair."

Taylor's head fell.

"I told you how that would be," he murmured at last. "I cannot feel that it is any proof of her innocence. Or rather," he added, "I should always have my doubts."

"And Mrs. Couldock and Miss Dawes?"

"Ah!" he cried, rising and turning away; "there is no question of marriage between either of them and myself."

I was therefore not astonished when the week went by and no announcement of his wedding appeared. But I was troubled and am troubled still, for if mistakes are made in criminal courts, and the innocent sometimes, through the sheer force of circumstantial evidence, are made to suffer for the guilty, might it not be that in this little question of morals Mrs. Walworth has been wronged, and that when I played the part of arbitrator in her fate, I only succeeded in separating two hearts whose right it was to be made happy?

It is impossible to tell, nor is time likely to solve the riddle. Must I then forever blame myself, or did I only do in this matter what any honest man would have done in my place? Answer me, some one, for I do not find my lonely bachelor life in any wise brightened by the doubt, and would be grateful to any one who would relieve me of it.

ABOUT THE AUTHOR

Anna Katharine Green (November 11, 1846 – April 11, 1935) was an American poet and novelist. She was one of the first writers of detective fiction in America and distinguished herself by writing well plotted, legally accurate stories (no doubt assisted by her lawyer father).

Born in Brooklyn, New York, Green's early ambition was to write romantic verse, and she corresponded with Ralph Waldo Emerson. When her poetry failed to gain recognition, she produced her first and best known novel, The Leavenworth Case (1878). She became a bestselling author, eventually publishing about 40 books.

Green was in some ways a progressive woman for her time—succeeding in a genre dominated by male writers—but she did not approve of many of her feminist contemporaries, and she was opposed to women's suffrage.

Green married the actor, and later designer and artist, Charles Rohlfs on November 25, 1884. They had one daughter and two sons, Roland Rohlfs and Sterling Rohlfs, who were test pilots. Green died in Buffalo, New York, at the age of 88.

Choose from Thousands of 1stWorldLibrary Classics By

A. M. Barnard
Ada Leverson
Adolphus William Ward
Aesop
Agatha Christie
Alexander Aaronsohn
Alexander Kielland
Alexandre Dumas
Alfred Gatty
Alfred Ollivant
Alice Duer Miller
Alice Turner Curtis
Alice Dunbar
Allen Chapman
Alleyne Ireland
Ambrose Bierce
Amelia E. Barr
Amory H. Bradford
Andrew Lang
Andrew McFarland Davis
Andy Adams
Angela Brazil
Anna Alice Chapin
Anna Sewell
Annie Besant
Annie Hamilton Donnell
Annie Payson Call
Annie Roe Carr
Annonaymous
Anton Chekhov
Archibald Lee Fletcher
Arnold Bennett
Arthur C. Benson
Arthur Conan Doyle
Arthur M. Winfield
Arthur Ransome
Arthur Schnitzler
Arthur Train
Atticus
B.H. Baden-Powell
B. M. Bower
B. C. Chatterjee
Baroness Emmuska Orczy
Baroness Orczy
Basil King
Bayard Taylor
Ben Macomber
Bertha Muzzy Bower
Bjornstjerne Bjornson

Booth Tarkington
Boyd Cable
Bram Stoker
C. Collodi
C. E. Orr
C. M. Ingleby
Carolyn Wells
Catherine Parr Traill
Charles A. Eastman
Charles Amory Beach
Charles Dickens
Charles Dudley Warner
Charles Farrar Browne
Charles Ives
Charles Kingsley
Charles Klein
Charles Hanson Towne
Charles Lathrop Pack
Charles Romyn Dake
Charles Whibley
Charles Willing Beale
Charlotte M. Braeme
Charlotte M. Yonge
Charlotte Perkins Stetson
Clair W. Hayes
Clarence Day Jr.
Clarence E. Mulford
Clemence Housman
Confucius
Coningsby Dawson
Cornelis DeWitt Wilcox
Cyril Burleigh
D. H. Lawrence
Daniel Defoe
David Garnett
Dinah Craik
Don Carlos Janes
Donald Keyhoe
Dorothy Kilner
Dougan Clark
Douglas Fairbanks
E. Nesbit
E. P. Roe
E. Phillips Oppenheim
E. S. Brooks
Earl Barnes
Edgar Rice Burroughs
Edith Van Dyne
Edith Wharton

Edward Everett Hale
Edward J. O'Biren
Edward S. Ellis
Edwin L. Arnold
Eleanor Atkins
Eleanor Hallowell Abbott
Eliot Gregory
Elizabeth Gaskell
Elizabeth McCracken
Elizabeth Von Arnim
Ellem Key
Emerson Hough
Emilie F. Carlen
Emily Bronte
Emily Dickinson
Enid Bagnold
Enilor Macartney Lane
Erasmus W. Jones
Ernie Howard Pie
Ethel May Dell
Ethel Turner
Ethel Watts Mumford
Eugene Sue
Eugenie Foa
Eugene Wood
Eustace Hale Ball
Evelyn Everett-green
Everard Cotes
F. H. Cheley
F. J. Cross
F. Marion Crawford
Fannie E. Newberry
Federick Austin Ogg
Ferdinand Ossendowski
Fergus Hume
Florence A. Kilpatrick
Fremont B. Deering
Francis Bacon
Francis Darwin
Frances Hodgson Burnett
Frances Parkinson Keyes
Frank Gee Patchin
Frank Harris
Frank Jewett Mather
Frank L. Packard
Frank V. Webster
Frederic Stewart Isham
Frederick Trevor Hill
Frederick Winslow Taylor

Friedrich Kerst
Friedrich Nietzsche
Fyodor Dostoyevsky
G.A. Henty
G.K. Chesterton
Gabrielle E. Jackson
Garrett P. Serviss
Gaston Leroux
George A. Warren
George Ade
Geroge Bernard Shaw
George Cary Eggleston
George Durston
George Ebers
George Eliot
George Gissing
George MacDonald
George Meredith
George Orwell
George Sylvester Viereck
George Tucker
George W. Cable
George Wharton James
Gertrude Atherton
Gordon Casserly
Grace E. King
Grace Gallatin
Grace Greenwood
Grant Allen
Guillermo A. Sherwell
Gulielma Zollinger
Gustav Flaubert
H. A. Cody
H. B. Irving
H.C. Bailey
H. G. Wells
H. H. Munro
H. Irving Hancock
H. R. Naylor
H. Rider Haggard
H. W. C. Davis
Haldeman Julius
Hall Caine
Hamilton Wright Mabie
Hans Christian Andersen
Harold Avery
Harold McGrath
Harriet Beecher Stowe
Harry Castlemon
Harry Coghill
Harry Houidini

Hayden Carruth
Helent Hunt Jackson
Helen Nicolay
Hendrik Conscience
Hendy David Thoreau
Henri Barbusse
Henrik Ibsen
Henry Adams
Henry Ford
Henry Frost
Henry James
Henry Jones Ford
Henry Seton Merriman
Henry W Longfellow
Herbert A. Giles
Herbert Carter
Herbert N. Casson
Herman Hesse
Hildegard G. Frey
Homer
Honore De Balzac
Horace B. Day
Horace Walpole
Horatio Alger Jr.
Howard Pyle
Howard R. Garis
Hugh Lofting
Hugh Walpole
Humphry Ward
Ian Maclaren
Inez Haynes Gillmore
Irving Bacheller
Isabel Cecilia Williams
Isabel Hornibrook
Israel Abrahams
Ivan Turgenev
J.G.Austin
J. Henri Fabre
J. M. Barrie
J. M. Walsh
J. Macdonald Oxley
J. R. Miller
J. S. Fletcher
J. S. Knowles
J. Storer Clouston
J. W. Duffield
Jack London
Jacob Abbott
James Allen
James Andrews
James Baldwin

James Branch Cabell
James DeMille
James Joyce
James Lane Allen
James Lane Allen
James Oliver Curwood
James Oppenheim
James Otis
James R. Driscoll
Jane Abbott
Jane Austen
Jane L. Stewart
Janet Aldridge
Jens Peter Jacobsen
Jerome K. Jerome
Jessie Graham Flower
John Buchan
John Burroughs
John Cournos
John F. Kennedy
John Gay
John Glasworthy
John Habberton
John Joy Bell
John Kendrick Bangs
John Milton
John Philip Sousa
John Taintor Foote
Jonas Lauritz Idemil Lie
Jonathan Swift
Joseph A. Altsheler
Joseph Carey
Joseph Conrad
Joseph E. Badger Jr
Joseph Hergesheimer
Joseph Jacobs
Jules Vernes
Julian Hawthrone
Julie A Lippmann
Justin Huntly McCarthy
Kakuzo Okakura
Karle Wilson Baker
Kate Chopin
Kenneth Grahame
Kenneth McGaffey
Kate Langley Bosher
Kate Langley Bosher
Katherine Cecil Thurston
Katherine Stokes
L. A. Abbot
L. T. Meade

L. Frank Baum
Latta Griswold
Laura Dent Crane
Laura Lee Hope
Laurence Housman
Lawrence Beasley
Leo Tolstoy
Leonid Andreyev
Lewis Carroll
Lewis Sperry Chafer
Lilian Bell
Lloyd Osbourne
Louis Hughes
Louis Joseph Vance
Louis Tracy
Louisa May Alcott
Lucy Fitch Perkins
Lucy Maud Montgomery
Luther Benson
Lydia Miller Middleton
Lyndon Orr
M. Corvus
M. H. Adams
Margaret E. Sangster
Margret Howth
Margaret Vandercook
Margaret W. Hungerford
Margret Penrose
Maria Edgeworth
Maria Thompson Daviess
Mariano Azuela
Marion Polk Angellotti
Mark Overton
Mark Twain
Mary Austin
Mary Catherine Crowley
Mary Cole
Mary Hastings Bradley
Mary Roberts Rinehart
Mary Rowlandson
M. Wollstonecraft Shelley
Maud Lindsay
Max Beerbohm
Myra Kelly
Nathaniel Hawthrone
Nicolo Machiavelli
O. F. Walton
Oscar Wilde

Owen Johnson
P.G. Wodehouse
Paul and Mabel Thorne
Paul G. Tomlinson
Paul Severing
Percy Brebner
Percy Keese Fitzhugh
Peter B. Kyne
Plato
Quincy Allen
R. Derby Holmes
R. L. Stevenson
R. S. Ball
Rabindranath Tagore
Rahul Alvares
Ralph Bonehill
Ralph Henry Barbour
Ralph Victor
Ralph Waldo Emmerson
Rene Descartes
Ray Cummings
Rex Beach
Rex E. Beach
Richard Harding Davis
Richard Jefferies
Richard Le Gallienne
Robert Barr
Robert Frost
Robert Gordon Anderson
Robert L. Drake
Robert Lansing
Robert Lynd
Robert Michael Ballantyne
Robert W. Chambers
Rosa Nouchette Carey
Rudyard Kipling
Saint Augustine
Samuel B. Allison
Samuel Hopkins Adams
Sarah Bernhardt
Sarah C. Hallowell
Selma Lagerlof
Sherwood Anderson
Sigmund Freud
Standish O'Grady
Stanley Weyman
Stella Benson
Stella M. Francis

Stephen Crane
Stewart Edward White
Stijn Streuvels
Swami Abhedananda
Swami Parmananda
T. S. Ackland
T. S. Arthur
The Princess Der Ling
Thomas A. Janvier
Thomas A Kempis
Thomas Anderton
Thomas Bailey Aldrich
Thomas Bulfinch
Thomas De Quincey
Thomas Dixon
Thomas H. Huxley
Thomas Hardy
Thomas More
Thornton W. Burgess
U. S. Grant
Upton Sinclair
Valentine Williams
Various Authors
Vaughan Kester
Victor Appleton
Victor G. Durham
Victoria Cross
Virginia Woolf
Wadsworth Camp
Walter Camp
Walter Scott
Washington Irving
Wilbur Lawton
Wilkie Collins
Willa Cather
Willard F. Baker
William Dean Howells
William le Queux
W. Makepeace Thackeray
William W. Walter
William Shakespeare
Winston Churchill
Yei Theodora Ozaki
Yogi Ramacharaka
Young E. Allison
Zane Grey